Erik's Story

Linda Kay Thompson

Illustrated by Erik David Behnke

Publication Consultants — Since 1978

PO Box 221974 Anchorage, Alaska 99522-1974
books@publicationconsultants.com—www.publicationconsultants.com

ISBN 978-1-59433-058-2
Library of Congress Catalog Card Number: 2007926126

Linda's New Book
It's Okay Mom

Dream Big And Make It Happen

Check Out What's Happening
www.brownbearproducts.biz or www.erikbehnke.com
Learn about Erik, Chris, and Linda today,
Progress with Erik's art,
This years events,
Plus the latest cards, prints,
poster, books, and more.

Manufactured in the United States of America.

Dedication

To my children, Erik and Chris, the loves of my life.
May you both have many more adventures.

Acknowledgments

I thank Linda Rutledge for the endless hours spent at my side as I struggled to teach at Kenny Lake School. She became a wonderful lifelong friend in the process.

Thank you Cheryl Kelly, my sister, for listening to my stories and encouraging me to write them down. Your continual love and support over the years that I have been a single mother have carried me though all the best and worst of times.

Thanks Erik David Behnke for working so hard at your art and providing me with a story that needs to be shared with other parents like me.

Special thanks to Christopher Ray Behnke for being a loving son and brother. Without your love and assistance, I never would have had the time to write in the first place.

Many thanks Reed Carlson and Byron Rice for believing that I could do the job you offered me and allowing me to dream big.

Thank you Ann Keffer, Kathleen Wright, and Rebecca Goodrich for editing and helping me make this book become a reality.

Chapter One
Frustration

I sat crying in the old rocker, creaking back and forth, while looking blindly toward the pure white cathedral ceiling far over head. My life wasn't working out. It was the beginning of August, 1997, school would start soon and I had once again been rejected for a teaching position. The district hired a twenty-two year old blond right out of college with no experience. There was a teacher glut and I couldn't compete with the young. I was considered old (49), too experienced, too well-educated, so too expensive to hire. I was miserable to the point of doubting my ability, and thus ruining my interviews. On top of it all, I didn't like what was happening at my boy's high school.

"God," I prayed, "Help me get out of this mess. I'll go wherever you want."

Four years before I had left Bush Alaska where I had had a good job as a teacher. I sold everything, took the money, flew to Palmer and built our 3,600 square foot super-insulated solar home of my design, with all the amenities. There was electricity, running water, a whirlpool bath, three greenhouses, two garages, a huge garden and much more. On the outside we looked like we lacked nothing.

In the Bush my two boys had grown up with most of their friends being Eskimo, Indian and Aleut but the two were always outsiders. They didn't look, act or speak like their classmates. Erik was sixteen and had Down's syndrome. Christopher was ten and was hearing impaired. Fortunately he was very smart and people rarely realized he was reading their lips. The Bush had been a safe place for them to grow up but by 1993 Erik was ready for high school and Chris for junior high. It was time to move where they would fit in and I could conveniently go shopping. Palmer was perfect, only 35 miles by car to the largest city in the state. I thought I would surely get a job but never did.

I sat there rocking. I secretly wiped the tears away, and tried to enjoy my beautiful home with its white walls, white carpets, and beautiful wood beams supporting the loft where Erik happily played with his toys and color markers. Chris, a tall blond handsome young man, was lounging on the couch reading a book. I said, "I know you love living in Palmer, but I need to start to think about my retirement. I'm 49 and I really need a contract to work toward it. I want to have retirement set up before I'm 65."

"Are you thinking about Bush teaching again?"

"I'm not applying for the Bush, but I'm thinking about it," I answered. "If I had a contract this year, I could retire by 63. We would also have some money for a change, instead of just scraping by each month. We all need checkups with the dentist and eye doctor. It all costs."

"Whatever you decide, Mom," Chris said.

He was wonderful. He knew that I had left a high paying Bush job so he and his brother could be happy in Palmer. It was a gamble that I had taken, and I lost that game. Deep down, I knew that life was not a gamble. There must be some reason I couldn't get a permanent job. There had to be some kind of plan in effect, but darn if I could see any reason in it.

During that summer of 1997, when the public schools were closed, I happily worked at the Alaska Job Corps as a substitute teacher. The pay was better and I loved the variety of jobs. I was working four or five days a week in everything from reading, math, and GED (General Education Diploma), to carpentry, heavy equipment, electrical, painting, business and accounting. Though I had work experience in all the above (except heavy equipment) I didn't qualify for any Corps contracted teaching positions. It seemed that I would be a substitute teacher for the rest of my life.

It was frustrating that I had no future, no insurance, and no sick leave, but even so, we had a lot to be grateful for. It was warm in August, I was debt free, the garden was in full bloom and I harvested fresh food by the basketfuls. Friends had given us fresh moose, caribou, and world-class Copper River salmon, which I quickly froze. My freezer was filling up fast for the winter. I endured my situation because we had a wonderful home and we were far from hungry. I had reached a point of accepting my fate, and though I really wanted change, I was still making no physical steps toward it. I had applied nowhere other than Palmer.

A few weeks later I was assigned to be the teacher in the accounting class at the Corps. I had to wear a business suit, high heels, nylons, makeup, and jewelry for the two-day job. The week before I had felt much more comfortable wearing steel toe boots, blue jeans, hard hat and heavy tool belt as I taught the Corps carpentry class how to shingle a roof.

"Ms. Thompson, phone," said the student secretary in the accounting class.

I went into the office and picked up the phone, "Hello, Linda Thompson speaking."

"Hello, my name is Reed Carlson. I am the principal at Kenny Lake School, Copper River School District. I have an opening for a special education teacher at our school and was wondering if you are certified in the subject."

As he spoke, I quickly got a piece of paper and started taking notes: REED CARLSON, Kenny Lake School, special ed. I have always been horrible with names and knew I would forget everything if I didn't write it down.

"Yes sir. I am also a certified secondary physical education teacher, elementary classroom teacher, and an elementary physical education teacher. I have four endorsements with the State of Alaska."

"Would you be interested in teaching in the Copper River School District?" he asked. "The position is in Kenny Lake. Do you know where that is?"

"Yes, sir, Kenny Lake school is south of Glennallen about fifty miles. I interviewed for a position there in 1987 and was offered a contract, but I went to South Naknek School that year, out west in Bristol Bay area. I would be interested in teaching at Kenny Lake School. Tell me more about the position."

"It is a K-12 special education position," he said. "Tell me about you."

I quickly summarized my life as junior/senior high school physical education teacher, elementary teacher, principal teacher, and elementary physical education teacher. I explained that I had just finished my endorsement in special education from University of Alaska, Anchorage. I stated that I was a parent of two special needs children and that I had twenty years of experience if you counted that. I also threw in my involvement in Special Olympics Alaska and my years as an advocate for people with disabilities with the Governor's Council and Hope Cottages while I lived in Dillingham. He seemed quite interested. I was bubbling over and had a hard time sitting on my chair in the office. My rear kept sliding off the edge. Here was a man who saw what I had to offer a school. It was wonderful to be desired after four years of rejection. I amazingly felt no self-doubt!

"How did you find me at the Alaska Job Corps Center?"

"I found your name on a list of unemployed special education teachers in Alaska. Then I found your home number and talked to your son Chris. He sounded like a very nice young man. He told me where you were working today. It took the Job Corps operator a while to find out where you were, but eventually we were connected," Mr. Carlson said. "Are you interested in applying for this opening?"

"Sure. It's on the road." Getting a job in a town on one of Alaska's few highways was exactly what I needed at that time. I didn't want to go back out in the Bush where we had to fly everywhere. I couldn't pass up this interview. "What do you need from me?"

"School starts next week, so we're going to do the interviews and hire this week. How about if you fax information about yourself?" He gave me the number.

"No problem. I have my resume. Do you want an Alaska Teacher Placement Center application? It might need a little updating, but it's basically accurate. I could fax everything including transcripts from all my colleges and a cover letter tomorrow morning at 8:30 a.m. I am scheduled to work this same position at the Job Corps, so I can have my accounting students fax it as part of their lessons."

"That's great. I will call tomorrow morning after the interview committee has reviewed the materials. Thanks."

"It's been great talking to you, Mr. Carlson."

I hung up the phone and started pacing around the little office. I wanted to scream with delight. I wanted the entire world to know about this call. I called home and thanked Chris for doing such a good job answering the phone. To hear it ringing, he must have been carrying it with him that day.

I felt like God was once again in charge of my life. Why for the past four years had I never felt this way? It seemed clear that God had heard my prayers. He was taking charge of everything, right down to getting me a job interview with a school district where I hadn't even applied. Was this what I was supposed to do? It seemed right. I decided to do my best and if the doors opened in that direction, we would go through them.

If this hiring committee wanted me, I would drop everything in

Palmer and move 225 miles east to the middle of nowhere. It was better than the Bush because it was on the road, very important in Alaska. That was enough. I could handle things. I would have to find a log cabin to live in, and we would go back to the camping mode of living again. Chris probably wouldn't remember the years of hauling wood and water, but Erik would. We would get by somehow.

Then I realized—insurance! We would have insurance! We could all go to the dentist again and Chris could get his eyes checked. He also needed new hearing aids. A regular, consistent paycheck—what a novel idea! I would like having one of those again.

All day, I was so excited that I could hardly maintain my composure with the job at hand. I managed to get through it, and at precisely 5 p.m. ran out to my Toyota truck, jumped in, and put the pedal to the metal. In ten minutes I was home, bubbling all over the boys.

Chris and Erik watched me gaily roar around the house. Neither knew what this could mean to them. They were truly happy for me. Erik sat in his loft, looking between the wood rails with a smile on his face, as I joyously told both boys about my day. He said nothing. Chris lay on the couch, smiling at me, and said little. He didn't really know what to say.

I knew we would lose the beautiful home when we had renters move into it. Life would certainly not be as easy as it had been for the past four years with water, toilets, whirlpool bathtub, and no woodstoves. I could justify the hardship I was about to take the family into. The easy living in Palmer had been the boys' years. Now it would be my turn. Besides I would have no problem withdrawing the boys from their high school. The experimental program was detrimental for Chris and I worried about Erik's future. I needed to be more involved to help him find a career. Change would be good.

"I know you have loved Palmer, boys, but now it's time for me to work toward a retirement."

"But what if you don't like it? Then what, Mom?" asked Chris.

"Once I sign a contract, I'm bound to it. We will have to stay for the entire school year. Besides, if I stay until January, I will be vested in the Alaska Teachers Retirement. At least I would have that."

"Church?" said Erik.

"We'll still have it. Chris and I will read the service like we did in the Bush. No more Sunday school in the Anchorage church anymore. Too far to drive."

"What about my friends?" he asked.

"We'll come home on weekends and holidays. You can see them then. Chris, I could stay here for a lifetime, just to be overlooked time and time again by this district. There are too many unemployed teachers in Palmer. I need at least one more year. Tell you what; if we don't like it, we could always come back to Palmer next summer."

The boys seemed open to the idea, so I went downstairs to my wonderfully white, clean bedroom, and dug out my brown leather briefcase with all my interview materials for Mr. Carlson. The following day I faxed all them to Kenny Lake School. It was sent by 8:35 a.m. Then it was a matter of waiting to see if he called back. Two hours later, Mr. Carlson called. I could hardly contain my joy, but I didn't want to alienate him with my excitement.

"Hello, this is Linda Thompson," I said, answering the accounting class phone.

"Hi, this is Reed Carlson. We have looked at your application, letters, transcripts and resume. We would like to interview you as soon as possible."

"I have tomorrow off, but I am booked here at the Corps on Thursday and Friday. Will that work for you?" I asked.

"That would be great. We will schedule interviews tomorrow. It will take you about four hours to drive here from Palmer. One o'clock would probably be the best time for you with the drive. Does that sound good for you?"

"Yes," I said. "I think we will drive that direction tonight after work and get a head start on the road. We own a camper. I'll need to bring my boys."

"Fine. Okay, I have you scheduled," he said. "See you tomorrow at one."

When I got off the phone I started thinking about what I would need to do after work: pack the camper with food and water, check engine fluids, check tires, fill the gas tank, and pack clothes, sleeping bags, interview dress, and, oh yes, curlers and makeup. I would have to look great, but not too great. I had to fit into the rural school while at the same time looking professional. I knew exactly the dress to wear. It was grey and black plaid. I would carry my briefcase with all the interview stuff in it. It was still ready from my last interview with Palmer, so all I needed to do was throw it in the camper.

I called Chris. He was by the phone again. "We are going to drive to Glennallen tonight after I get off work. Pack up anything you want to bring. Have your clothes ready when I get home and a couple of good books to read while we're gone."

"How long?" he asked.

"One or two days, max. I should go back to work at the Corps on Thursday. I'm scheduled to work in Commercial Painting again. Okay?"

"Sure, Mom."

"How is Erik doing?" I asked.

"He is in the loft, rocking and drawing as usual."

"Could I speak to him?" I asked.

"Sure." I could hear Chris walking up the wooden stairs to the loft. "Erik, here's Mom. Say hi."

I heard Erik clearing his throat, but he never said anything.

"Erik, this is Mom. Say hi," I said.

"Oh, it's Mom. Hi." His voice was soft and loving.

"Erik, we are going to go camping tonight in the camper. Okay?" I said. "When I get home, we will pack up the camper fast and leave. I just want you to know to pack up your books so they will be ready when you see me." I had learned over the years to pre-teach Erik. If I gave him a heads-up on changes in his schedule, he could cooperate more easily. It was well worth it to take the extra time.

"Oh boy, camping tonight!" he said. He loved to go camping.

"Okay, I had better get back to work. Bye," I said.

"Bye, Mom," he said. He put the phone down, but didn't turn it off. Chris picked it up and said, "You there, Mom?"

"Yes."

"Does it have a high school?" he asked.

"Yes. I don't know how many students there are, but I am sure it will have all the important classes you need for college. It'll be perfect. We will both take a look at it tomorrow, kid. If it doesn't look okay for you, I won't take the job. This has to bless all three of us, not just me."

I had raised my boys to be open to change. Chris had a bit of the desire for adventure that I had. As far as Erik was concerned, everything was fine as long as he had a floor on which to spread his precious favorite books, and tracing paper for his thousands of art tracings and that no one stepped on his stuff. I was grateful that I had been blessed with these wonderful boys. God was good to me as far as my children went. He knew what I needed.

"Okay. I'm happy for you, Mom," said Chris, and he truly meant it.

That night after work, we quickly prepped the van and left by 7:30 p.m. We drove until 11 when we arrived at Glennallen. I had the Alaska Milepost, the road guide for the Alcan Highway, Yukon, and Alaska. There was a state campground just north of Glennallen. It would be perfect; nice and quiet, off the highway, private, and yet other travelers would be nearby. We paid our $10 to park and went to bed. Erik and I slept in our down bags in the king size bed on top, and Chris took the twin bed below. It was very crowded, but comfortable. I tossed all night as pouring rain beat hard on the roof of the camper. I kept going over possible answers to questions that might be asked. When dawn broke about six a.m., I was exhausted. The rain was coming down even harder, but we were self-contained in the camper and only left to use the outhouses in the campground.

I was afraid that I would be late, so we left right after breakfast and drove down the Richardson Highway to the Edgerton Highway, and the last fifty miles to the school. As we drove, we noticed gravel and mud roads branching off into the woods with mailboxes next to the highway. Glennallen and Copper Center were the only little towns to be found. Kenny Lake School appeared alone.

The school was made up of five buildings, three of which were being used. There was one pinkish-beige two-classroom building, labeled "Kenny Lake Hawks" that had a big hawk painted on it. The second building was an old, beige school building that looked like three portable classrooms all somehow attached to each other. The third and most impressive building was the high school. It had pea-green metal siding with a beige roof. From the camper I could see one classroom, a high roof designed for a gymnasium, and an office. Most of the classrooms were out of view so I couldn't tell how many there actually were.

Erik had claimed the front of the camper and had the dashboard covered with piles of his books. He was working in a coloring book, using a new set of markers. His favorite colors were already starting to dry up. But he wouldn't complain, just made do with what he had left.

I parked far away from the high school, as if I were a tourist. I didn't want to leave the camper until I was totally ready and it was time to walk in the door. I put on my interview dress, make-up, and high-heeled shoes. I took out a cooking pot and boiled my curlers until they were hot enough to bend my straight hair and not burn it. Finally I was ready. "Well, how do I look, boys?"

Chris was lying on the top bunk of the camper, studying Highland bagpipe music. When he tired of playing his chanter, he looked at me for a minute. "Great, Mom. When you are done, can we look around the school?" Chris asked.

"Absolutely. I will take both of you around," I said.

"Good luck, Mom."

I drove the camper the 75 yards to the high school and parked it as close to the door as possible.

"Okay," I said. "Time's up. Here I go. I love you boys."

Chapter Two
The Interview

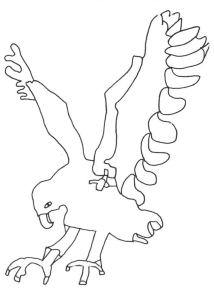

It was still raining. I left the camper without a raincoat. I held my briefcase over my head and ran into the school building as quickly as possible and I hardly got a hair of my freshly curled head wet. Test #1, getting in the building still looking okay. On to Test #2, the interview.

I was greeted by several people at the door. I didn't know who they were, but later I learned they were Carla Scherholdt, 2-3rd grade teacher; Felicia Riedel, 4-5th grade teacher; Reed Carlson, principal; Marlene Roig, SpEd. Aide; Sharon Lain, librarian; and the superintendent of Copper River Schools. The committee members took turns asking me questions. I had learned before to answer all questions quickly, and to stay on the point. I tried hard not to get off on a tangent. The interview went fine. I experienced no frustration at all as I had in Palmer and was feeling quite confident for a change. Finally, they asked if I had any questions.

"Yes, I have a fourteen-year-old son that I hope will be able to go to college. Tell me what you have to offer him in classes that will prepare him for that future."

"We have biology, sciences, algebra, geometry, algebra II, English, history, physical education, foreign languages, band, aviation ground school, and home economics," Reed said. "We're also trying to set up an art and woodshop program."

Some classes were offered right in Kenny Lake School with teachers in the building. Some of the classes were by interactive television between Glennallen High School and Kenny Lake School. If the teacher was in Kenny Lake, they could broadcast from little Kenny Lake School, with other students in a classroom in Glennallen watching as he or she lectured. Sometimes the teacher might broadcast from Glennallen School to Kenny Lake School. Seemed like a good idea to me.

Next I asked, "If I get this job, what will it entail?"

"You would teach special education in both the elementary school across the parking lot, and in the junior-senior high school. Your classroom would be in the Kenny Lake Hawk building in the elementary school and your 20 to 25 students would be grades K-12. Marlene Roig would be one of your aides, and another aide, Linda Rutledge, does mostly speech. We might ask you to teach one physical education class."

"That sounds like a great job. I would enjoy the variety of teaching both physical education and special education."

The superintendent said, "School starts on Monday. Do you think you could start that quickly?"

"Yes. I could live in my camper while I hunted for a place to live."

Then the superintendent made a joke. "Now, that could be a problem. There is no place here to live that has running water, and you'll have to chop wood." He laughed a deep laugh and with a mischievous smile on his face.

I thought he was joking. With all the roads branching off the highway, how could there not be a place for us to live? Maybe he had an odd sense of humor. I certainly would be able to rent whatever we needed. It was worth whatever it cost because with my last half-year in, I would be vested in the retirement system. I could handle whatever life threw my way. I was certain that he was teasing me. I wasn't going to get suckered into thinking we wouldn't have what we needed.

I wasn't sure how the committee felt about me, but I was very happy with their answers. I'd make sure that Erik's program would be great. It sounded like Christopher's program would also be more than adequate. It actually sounded more academic than what he had at Palmer High. I was quite happy with what this rural school had to offer my family.

After the interview was over, I asked if it would be all right if I brought in my boys and showed them around the school. Everyone thought that was a great idea. I went out to the van in the rain and talked to the boys about coming in. Chris hopped down from the top of the camper, and together we were able to get Erik out of the front seat.

"How did it go, Mom?" Chris asked excitedly.

"I don't know. I think it went okay. I spoke the truth. Maybe they won't like that. There are many ways to look at teaching. Don't worry. Look at today as an adventure. This place will have some advantages for you over the big Palmer schools. We'll see if they want me. I'll tell you, if they offer me a job, I'll take it.

Another thing I really like is that I can be Erik's teacher for the first time. Ever since Palmer High told me that Erik could fold towels for a career after graduation, I've wanted more for him. I have some art ideas I really want to try out."

The interview committee greeted my boys with loving kindness that I hadn't felt anywhere before. People shook Chris' hand and treated him like an adult. Erik was treated also with respect, joy, and honest love. There was no looking down on my family. It felt like we were being accepted into a new and loving family, like going home for the first time. I wanted the job more than ever. The love I felt was incredibly wonderful.

The boys and I looked into the tiny classrooms. Where the interview took place there was a table, chairs, and a TV. It was the interactive TV classroom where foreign language and aviation ground school were taught. There was a very small social studies classroom/home economics room and an English classroom. Both rooms were little and had about twenty desks crammed in them. Teacher desks were each surrounded with file cabinets, shelves of books and supplies. There wasn't enough storage in either room for the teacher. "With rooms this small, I'll tell you one thing, Chris. You'll get lots of personal attention," I whispered.

Chris smiled, "Okay with me."

Science was taught in a complex of two classrooms, one for labs and one for lectures. Between the classrooms was an office with glass windows so at all times the teacher could keep an eye on what was happening in both sections. The computer classroom had fifteen new Macintosh computers with Internet capability, something I had just heard about that summer while at the Corps. Upstairs was a large math classroom with about twenty desks. All the rooms had lots of windows. Last was the library. Its wall of south-facing windows looked out on the future track. It was a small library with two rows of bookshelves in the center of the room and books along the walls. It had a little bit of everything.

The north side of the building was a kitchen that doubled as the school cafeteria and home economics classroom. Then there was the gym. It had a very firm floor made of blue foam. It was slightly larger than a basketball court. There were some folding bleachers about eight seats high on the east wall. High on the walls were giant handmade paper letters saying "Seize The Day" and "Make Every Second Count." Positive motivation; I liked it. Last was the shop. It had a drill press, planer, table saw, workbenches, and lots of tools on the shelves. The school had everything we needed. It was perfect for my boys.

Teachers were already at work getting ready for school. Their classrooms were totally turned upside down with reorganization and planning for the new year. The dedication of the staff was something one felt immediately on entering the school. This school wasn't only a job, it was family, it was home, and it was their life. I had never seen a school staff that worked so well together. I wanted to be part of the team.

I wasn't offered a contract at that time, since others had to be interviewed and my references checked. The boys and I were soon back in the camper, heading back to Palmer.

"Chris, did you like it?"

"Sure, Mom. It seemed okay. It would be great if you got a job. I know you want it."

"I know you'll miss your friends, but I'm sure we'll drive to Palmer and Anchorage often."

I felt guilty. It was more than tearing him away from his friends. Chris loved the arts. When he was a young child, I had helped with elementary school plays, even written them, so he could act, something he loved to do. When we moved to Palmer, the Valley Performing Arts group was only four miles from home. He always landed fun parts in the children's plays. It was wonderful to see him on stage. He loved performance. In eighth and ninth grades, he focused more on learning to play his bagpipes with the Alaska Highlanders. He was progressing rapidly. Kenny Lake wasn't the place for a child who was interested in performing arts. We'd have to make do.

"We'll have to find out if there are any other Scottish Highland pipe players in the Copper River area with whom you could practice. Hey, Kenny Lake School will be a great place for you. You won't have to play outside or in the greenhouse. On nights and weekends, I bet we can get you in the warm gymnasium so you can practice whenever you want."

I was trying to get him excited about the idea of living there. He was excited for me and open to the concept of moving again, but he didn't know what it all meant in the big scheme of things.

Erik happily read his books in the back of the camper. I drove on, hour after hour, through miles of empty taiga and on to narrow winding roads through the hills and mountain pass from Gunsight Mountain to Matanuska Glacier to Sutton and, finally, Palmer. I was so excited at the idea of getting a job that I had to concentrate at being a careful driver. My mind was already working on how to pack up and move an entire household in four days. It would have been easy to drive off the narrow road when going around the sharp turns of the mountainsides if my speed picked up.

I was very happy to get home that night, stretch out, and sleep in my beautiful room with its white walls, its white carpet, my antique walnut bed covered with the homemade blue log cabin quilt, and my delicate two-tiered round table and dresser.

Thursday, while working in Painting at the Corps, I got another call from Kenny Lake.

"Hello, this is Reed Carlson. I have checked your references, and we would like to offer you a contract to teach special education at Kenny Lake School. Would you like to sign it?" he asked.

"Yes, sir, I would," I answered.

"Good. Can you begin on Monday with the others? It will be a preplanning workday. After work, you can drive to Glennallen and sign your contract."

How wonderful to think that I finally would have a contracted position. I was leaving the humiliation of Palmer schools behind me.

The rest of the day, while keeping an eye on my students as they practiced putting plaster on the practice boards and painting projects in the shop, I thought about what I had done. I was on another roller coaster ride emotionally. When was I going to learn to just settle down and be happy where I was? I was looking at a new, unknown future. What would Kenny Lake have to offer me besides just a job? It was noted for being even colder than Fairbanks. That meant it could get down to fifty even sixty degrees below zero. The school and its staff seemed perfect but I was giving up on my beautiful 3,600-square-foot luxury home with its wonderful gardens and greenhouses. I was going back out in the Bush—part way anyway. Certainly the superintendent was just teasing me about the wood and water problems. At least I would be able to drive out whenever I wanted to get to civilization. Its accessibility made it a big step up from Dillingham, but it would be a definite step down in housing from Palmer.

While driving home from work, I began to cry. What had I done? I was being selfish about my needs for retirement. How could I even think about moving my boys in one weekend? It was going to be hard. Once home I just sat around the house and looked at the piles of stuff that I needed to pack. For once, I wished I was still married to Steve so he could help me. But I had no one.

Erik spent Thursday evening in the loft, next to the balcony. I went upstairs to watch him and think about our future. He was sitting in his favorite corner on the immaculate white carpet with all his books, hundreds of tracings and favorite videos in neat piles all around him. The drawers to the dresser were opened slightly so he could see inside them where he had stacked his hundreds of tracings. There were plastic milk crates filled with stuffed toys, tracing paper, and lots of felt tip marker boxes.

I walked over to him and sat down on the floor to watch. "Erik, do you understand that we are moving to Kenny Lake this week?"

He was closely studying a cartoon, using binoculars backwards. He liked looking at how cartoon art was done. He put them down.

"What?" he asked.

""We are moving again."

"Why?"

"Because Mom needs a job. You know that school we went to yesterday, the one where it rained so hard? Remember, you went inside to see the school."

"Oh, yes."

"So do you understand that we are moving again?" I asked him.

His eyes were focused off in the distance. He didn't understand what I was asking.

"Is it okay with you, Erik, if we move again?" I asked.

"Okay," he said. He had answered, but didn't know what I was asking of him. He took up his favorite Disney book, *Pocahontas*, and started to trace it again. He loved that story. He started rocking back and forth as he returned to his imagination where he was most happy. Real life was too complicated. Erik, my twenty-year-old, couldn't help.

I didn't go to work at the Job Corps on Friday. I resigned on Thursday afternoon and explained about my new job. During the three-day weekend, Chris tried to be helpful for short periods. His priorities were different from mine. All he wanted on weekends was to play Dungeons and Dragons with his high school buddies.

I asked him to pack up his room, he answered,

"But, Mom, nobody here is going to school for two more weeks. I would rather stay here and see my friends until school starts."

"But we will be living in Kenny Lake; school starts earlier there. I can't leave you here. You aren't old enough yet. You have to go with me."

"But I want to see the guys. They are playing Dragon Raid at the clubhouse tonight and I want to go. I can pack tomorrow."

I had tried so hard to keep Chris out of drugs and alcohol. His only vice was this game. All his friends played it, so he wanted to.

I could argue with Chris, but he didn't listen. He had a way of turning off conversations that he didn't want to hear so that my voice just went right on by him. He was very chaotic and disorganized. He didn't have a sense of how long it would take to pack up and move. Neither did I at that time. All I knew was, I was totally overwhelmed. My buddy Chris was no help.

I finally called Steve's mom, Peggy Behnke. I explained the job in detail to her. "I'm so happy that I got this job. It will be perfect."

"When do you start work?"

"Monday."

"That's fast. Do you want to leave Erik here with me for the semester or school year?"

"No. I'll be Erik's teacher and will finally be able to have the kind of program that I want for him."

"Are you packing now?" she asked.

"I'm trying, but I'm torn. I don't want to leave my beautiful home, but I really want the job. I need to think about retirement. I'm not getting any younger." My eyes started to fill with tears, and I had a hard time speaking. She picked up on my desperation and frustration.

"How about if you leave both boys with Mel and me, until you're ready for them. You have a couple of teacher work days before you start with students, don't you?"

"Yes."

"The boys can miss a couple of school days. They'll be okay. You just pack enough for them for the week and I'll bring them to you Friday night after school."

Suddenly my spirits soared. I was free to go on an adventure without worrying about the men in my life. Grandma would take care of both of them. I could find a place to live, figure out my new job, and enjoy the new experience instead of feeling overwhelmed—at least I'd be less overwhelmed.

"Sounds like the perfect solution. I can go ahead, pack up my school materials, camping gear, clothes for work, food, and water and drive the camper to Kenny Lake Sunday afternoon after I deliver the boys to you. Thank you!" I had a lot for which to be grateful. I really needed help, and Peggy and Mel were there for me. How many ex-in-laws would help an ex-daughter-in-law like they did? "Let me talk to the boys about it and I'll call you back." I went to find Chris.

He was lying on the couch, totally engrossed in one of his favorite books of the summer. He had already reread *The Hobbit* and was now enjoying *The Lord of the Rings* trilogy again. Books of this nature were a love and he devoured them. The Palmer Public Library never had enough to satisfy his desires.

"Chris, I know you don't want to go to Kenny Lake this week. I understand, I wouldn't either if I were you. There won't be any school for a few days. I don't like the idea of you staying here alone. If you want to stay, you can stay at the homestead," I said.

"Mom, I don't want to go. Can't I stay with my friends in Palmer?"

"No. You have the choice of Grandma's or Kenny Lake."

One thing I was learning about Chris, he was not as easy as Erik now that he was a teenager. In his younger years, he was happy and easygoing. Something happened in junior high when he was thirteen. With time, I realized he was trying to become independent. All the boys were changing that way. They needed their moms, but like young eagles, they were trying out their wings. He was trying to fly.

Every weekend I'd hear, "But, Mom, Dragon Raid is a Christian version of Dungeons and Dragons. We are playing like we are fighting for the Lord. It's okay!"

I wasn't sure. Since I had never met those older men at the club house, and he wanted to maintain the appearance of being separate and independent from me, I thought it was wise to keep him reined in.

He grumbled, very unhappy with me, but finally said, "Okay, Grandma's."

Erik was always interested in going to the homestead and staying as long as I would let him. He loved hiking, canoeing, and the peace he found there. Grandma had a nice collection of Star Wars and Star Trek toys for him to play with and lots of tracing paper. He definitely wanted Grandma's.

I immediately called Peggy. With the boys safely in her care, I could focus on moving, but even after I knew I didn't have to worry about Chris and Erik, once in a while I would catch myself crying again. It was sad to give up on my dream getting a job in Palmer, and living in my beautiful house for the rest of my life. Life was a known factor in Palmer; Kenny Lake was full of unknowns.

Chapter Three
Starting Over

By Sunday, the camper was so full that I could barely get in. Even my sleeping bunk was full of heavy boxes. I ran a safety check on the lights, turn signals, oil, water, and propane for the rig. Lastly, I crawled on top of the boxes full of school materials and books, and packed the refrigerator and freezer with food for the week. All my boots and foul weather gear were hanging in the closet that doubled as a shower. It was fall in Kenny Lake, even though it was August. At any moment, it could get cold and snow there. On the other hand, it might even warm into the sixties. Alaska weather is not predictable.

I loaded up the boys in the red Toyota truck and drove to Wasilla, where I met Grandma at the Cottonwood Mall parking lot. I unloaded the suitcases while Erik and Chris took their bags of favorite books and things and put them in her yellow Blazer. I gave Erik a big hug, while he gave me a loving soft hug back. Chris grabbed me and tried to lift me off the ground. During this summer, he had passed me up both in height and weight. After setting me down, he picked up his bagpipes and hopped in the back seat. Erik always got to sit in the front when in Grandma's car. He was her first grandchild.

"Thanks, Peggy, for helping me this week." She gave me a hug. Then, I told each of the boys, "I love you." You never know how long you are going to be around so one thing was always important to me, that Chris and Erik knew their mother really loved them.

Erik replied, "Oh, okay."

Chris said, "I love you too, Mom." They drove off west as I waved good-bye.

I quickly drove back to the Palmer house, parked the truck in the garage, and started driving north and east in the grey Chevy van camper. After four years of stability, in a "normal" neighborhood, I was off. My new adventure was now beginning. Five hours later, I arrived at the school. I pulled the camper to an area on campus, surrounded by trees that would give me a little privacy. It was far from the playground and hockey rink, and was a fine place to park. I climbed over the boxes, pulled several out off my bunk, crawled into my sleeping bag and immediately fell asleep, exhausted.

Early the next morning, a car arrived. I peeked out the bunk window and noticed a short woman with blond hair get out. It was the school secretary. About seven, another car drove up, which I learned later was Irene Tansy's. When I saw Reed Carlson arrive, I got up, dressed, grabbed my shower bag with my towel, soap, brush, toothbrush and toothpaste; jumped out of the camper, and walked across the parking lot to the high school.

The blond secretary stood in the office. We were about the same age. She was sitting at her computer. "Good morning," I said. "I'm Linda Thompson, the new special education teacher."

"Hi, I'm Syvie Breivogel. Nice to meet you."

Reed Carlson walked into the office. "When did you get in last night?" he asked.

"Oh, about ten or eleven. My watch stopped. Not sure exactly. The sun had set, and it was almost dark when I parked over by the elementary school."

"Were you warm enough out there?" he asked.

"Oh, yes. It's a little crowded now though, since the van is packed with all my school things. I hope to unload today so I will have room to live in there this week. Is there a shower I can use?"

"Sure, in the gym, but heat's not on yet. I'm afraid it will be rather cold," he said. "We will probably turn it on in a couple of days." He gave me his keys so I could unlock the door.

Inside the tiny locker room, there were three shower heads in one open tiled area, a toilet, a sink, and a row of tall lockers that covered one fifteen-foot wall. Along another stretch of wall, there was a pegged wooden towel rack where students could hang their towels or clothes. It was so cold that I didn't want to undress. *This will be invigorating to say the least*, I thought. I hung up my clothes, and grabbed the soap. Leaving the towel on the floor, I stepped into the shower and I turned on the icy water. My heart started beating like a coughing engine. Shock! I jumped out, and soaped up, then jumped back in and rinsed off as quickly and thoroughly as possible, and turned off the water. I quickly dressed to stop the shivering reaction from the forty- to fifty-degree water and the fifty-degree locker room. I was ready for longjohns already and wondered if I would ever warm up, as I walked back to the office.

Reed gave me keys to my classroom and introduced me to Linda Rutledge, the speech and special education aide. She was about my age, and looked like she belonged back in the sixties. I could clearly picture her as a flower child at a love-in. She had long, dark-brown braids and wore baggy pants and a big baggy sweatshirt. She was wonderfully kind and amiable. I immediately knew, before we even left the building, that we were kindred spirits. We would be great friends and work together wonderfully as a team.

She took me over to the special education classroom, one of the two rooms in the Hawk building. The classroom was a big mess of desks, bulletin boards, tables, chairs, and file cabinets, all in a heap. Together, we looked around the room at all the materials. Then we opened the file cabinet that held the Individual Education Plans for the twenty-five students that might be mine that year and studied the plans together. I knew nothing about the students, and Linda was a wealth of information. But by the time I finished looking at all the plans, I wondered how I would ever keep them straight. I had to have some system. I couldn't keep the first graders and the high school students separate in my mind. They were just names.

"Let's just work on the organization of the classroom," I said. "How many high school students do we have? How many junior high, and elementary students?"

She helped me write a list so I had an approximate number from which to work. I learned that most of the elementary students would be served in the elementary mainstream classroom, with special education assistance on their assignments.

"So this will be more of a resource classroom with students coming and going each day?"

"Yes," said Linda.

I looked around. "This is a huge north-facing window. Then on the south side, there is just a little tiny one. I do love to sit by the window. It'll be cold in the winter over there, so let's put our desks there and the student desks in the middle of the room where it should be warmer."

"That sounds great," said Linda. We carried the two teacher desks individually across the room, together like a team. "How about the file cabinets?"

"I'll need the five drawer right by my desk since it will have all the records in it," I said. We tipped that cabinet onto a yellow cart, wedged another cart under the end of it, and moved it easily over by the desk. Once it was in place, we tipped the carts out and dumped the monstrously heavy file exactly where we wanted it.

"Would you help me empty the camper? I have boxes of books that we can put in our class library." There would be more when I packed up the Palmer house. Chris had outgrown many of his books, and Erik would love to have his books in this room so he could enjoy them during school. I drove the camper over to the door of the building, and we started to unload. Each carton weighed sixty- to seventy-pounds, but with Linda on one end and me on the other, it was easy. I found two bookshelves in the building and set them up on the south wall. Then we started to fill the shelves. By the end of the day, the furniture was mostly in place.

In the afternoon, Marlene Roig came by. Marlene was longest-employed in the Copper River School District and all-knowledgeable about academics. She was listed as my Chapter I Aide and would have about thirty students from kindergarten to ninth grade under her supervision. I quickly realized that she and Linda were very special aides. I felt we could do anything with this team of professionals.

Marlene and Linda took me next door. The building seemed to be several portable buildings chaotically arranged together and divided into four classrooms. Marlene's room had an entire thirty-foot wall of shelving to the ceiling, full of books, references, supplies, and art paper. You name it; Marlene had it, all very nicely organized. At least I wouldn't have to order anything to start the year.

I soon learned that if I wanted my students to grow in reading, I could get very sound advice from Marlene on what programs had been tried, would be best and where they could be located in the schools. She didn't have the degree or the certificate, but she knew far more than many teachers about reading. The entire school staff really appreciated her dedication. She was a role model for all.

Linda had years of experience and training to be a speech aide. Since most special education teachers are not certified in the subject, we had an itinerant teacher from Big Delta. She supervised Linda on how to do her job. One thing I had learned in my years of Bush teaching at South Naknek, was to trust my experienced aide. Just let them do their work. It was already obvious that Linda was very good at what she did.

At 3:30, I left for Glennallen. At 5, I met with the superintendent and the president of the school board and signed my contract. My salary took a $5,000 drop from Dillingham, but it certainly was better than the $20,000 I was making substituting year 'round in Palmer, which just barely covered everyday bills.

To celebrate, I went to Tastee Freez in Glennallen and had a chocolate malt and a burger. Then, it was back in the camper for the fifty-mile drive to Kenny Lake School and the parking lot. By the time I arrived, it was almost bedtime. I wouldn't have students the next day, so I could go to bed right away, without preparing lesson plans.

On Tuesday, I continued to clean and organize my classroom because on Wednesday we would have to go to Glennallen for teacher inservice. I worked nonstop to get it all together in time for my students on Thursday. Linda, Marlene and I divvied out jobs to make sure every student's IEP goals would be met as far as we could see at the time. We knew some goals would be missed, but by accurate record-keeping, we'd find those gaps and fix them by week two or three when all students were back in school. I took my responsibilities and they took theirs. From the start, we were a team.

On top of teaching all day, I had so much to learn and so much paperwork. There were lesson plans for students in twenty-two or more different directions, Individual Education Plans, referrals, evaluations, cover sheets, documentation of daily progress on each IEP goal and objective, and quarterly reports. Besides that, I had to manage K-12 resource and self-contained students in the same room, select educational materials that were best for each learning style and disability, communicate with the community of parents, and much more. Would I ever get it all straight?

I wanted everything organized and neat. It was hard to come into the program as a first-year special education teacher, though I had seven and a half years of teaching experience. Special ed. was certainly different because there was always the threat of lawsuits if things weren't done a certain way. I felt overwhelmed at the beginning, but as I outlined all the things I needed to master and started to check off things I had learned, I began to enjoy the week.

From the start, Linda cared about my family and me. She worked long hours after her paid day ended. She was very interested in Erik and Chris and the program we were about to start. I will never forget the second day when we were discussing all of our special education students. We had been working on examining our progress with every student's goals and objectives. We hadn't had a break for hours.

When we got to Erik, a name on a file folder only, I said, "Let's sit down for a minute and take a break." We sat down in blue plastic student chairs and leaned back, relaxed. I had my hands behind my head and my feet up on the wooden tabletop. I was tired from all the brain work.

Linda said," Tell me about Erik."

"Erik is twenty and has gone to high school for four years already," I said. "He's very difficult to hear. Used to have a loud voice, but now he whispers. It's getting harder to understand what he has to say. No one knows why. It's frustrating. He's very kind."

"Does he try hard in school?"

"I think so. Tests show he doesn't have a lot of potential and his IQ is only 36. He reads at about first or second grade level, but he used to read at third grade. I don't know why he doesn't now. He loves to please people and is very easy to work with. His math skills are about kindergarten level, I guess. I know he can't add two plus three but he can count. We'll have to see how high."

"I think I will enjoy getting to know him," she said.

"Our challenge will be figuring out a career for him. It was suggested in his last IEP meeting that he'd be great at working in a laundry because he is so neat and particular. But he loves to color things. He spends all of his free time reading simple books, looking at ads, tracing pictures out of them, and doing a great job of coloring things his way," I said. "He doesn't care what colors other people want things. He has his own way of adding color. It's fascinating to watch."

"What do you dream for him?" she asked.

I leaned back in my chair, and thought for a few seconds. *I certainly want more for my son than what the schools have offered us.* "I had dreamed for years that Erik would work for Walt Disney, and color cartoons. But that's impossible because all cartoons are now computerized. He doesn't like computers that much. He just likes to color. He wouldn't follow anyone else's color scheme anyway. You know, I'd like to see if he has any talent as an artist."

"Oh, that sounds exciting! I love art. It will be fun to work with him," said Linda.

"Great!"

"How do you want to start?" said Linda.

"I have been thinking he might be able to design cards. I have a couple of teacher friends that have their primary students design cards for fundraisers. Sounds like something that would work for Erik if he can draw. By golly, if they can do it, he sure can too. It'll take some research on the best way to print them."

"How will you sell them?" she asked.

"I used to be a furrier in Juneau and sold my wares to nine stores in Alaska. I know the tourist trade. I loved the sales part, but got really tired of making each individual item for sale. Fact is I still avoid sewing today. I went out of business and back to teaching in '87, suddenly. It was hard to work a 16 hour day and not make enough to support a family. Cards would be a much better product to make and sell. Less investment. We could have them commercially printed. Then we'd only have to package, advertise, and market."

"I know lots of places where he could sell them right here in this valley· shops and stores, the market," said Linda.

"We could go beyond the valley. We could try to market them all around the state in gift shops," I said. "Erik loves animals, so wildlife should keep his interest. It's also what the tourists want to buy to take home from their vacations. It'd be affordable, a part of Alaska, have a great story, fit in a suitcase, and not break."

"Sounds like a great idea! This sounds like fun to me. When do we start?" Linda was joining me in my outrageous dream for this lovable young man, and she hadn't even met him. This was the beginning of hundreds of hours of brainstorming. As we unpacked books, cleaned cupboards, washed desks, and organized everything, we continued to discuss what we would do when Erik arrived. The planning was in operation, and we didn't even know yet if he could draw.

Thursday and Friday were the first days of school. I spent my first day getting to know the students and testing them to find out what they needed to work on. As I matched students with IEPs (Individual Education Plans), things started to fit into my brain and make sense.

Thursday after school, I had my schedule coming along and had a good grasp of my lesson plans for the next week. As Linda hurried out the door at 5 p.m. in hopes of beating her husband home from work, she said, "Now don't stay too late."

"I'll try not to. I just need to finish my notes on the students and my lesson plans," I said.

"Promise you will leave before 9 p.m.," she called back from her truck as she warmed up the engine. "You work too hard!"

"I'll try. I really want to get driving as soon as possible tomorrow after school is out. If I work tonight, I won't have to stay late tomorrow."

"Okay, but try," she insisted.

"I will," I said, lying. Truth was I loved what I was doing and didn't want to quit. I waved goodbye and watched her drive across the gravel parking lot, leaving a cloud of dust behind her.

I was hungry. In the camper, I fixed a can of soup and a grilled cheese sandwich, and went back to the classroom.

Slowly, I was getting organized. By 8 p.m. I had reading programs figured out for my high school students, and I was all set up for junior high reading classes. After that, I focused my efforts on the following week's plans. There was still more I needed to know about some of the kids, but I had enough information to get a general plan together. At least now I knew which students I was supposed to be working with. With thirteen grade levels, I needed a plan to make sure I didn't overlook any student's needs. The plans gave me a bit of confidence.

On Friday morning, I registered Chris in all his classes: geometry, English 9/10, science, aviation ground school, and Intro Macintosh Applications. Teachers were already piling the homework on the students and it was only the second day of school. I had to get Chris to Kenny Lake on Monday. This school really pushed the academics. I was thrilled.

The entire first week I had camped in the school parking lot. By Friday, when the time came to drive back home to Palmer for the weekend of packing, I had not found a place to live. I had not even looked.

After the last of three buses headed out of the gravel parking lot, I did fifteen minutes of last-minute clean-up in my classroom. "Linda, I'm going home now," I called down the little hallway over the rattling, hissing furnace.

"You never did find a place to live," she said as she walked into the room.

"I know," I said guiltily.

"We'll go looking on Monday. I'll see what I can find for you over the weekend."

"That would be great, Linda." She walked out to the parking lot with me after we locked the doors. It felt odd to be leaving. I hadn't left the school grounds since I had arrived except to sign my contract and to go to inservice. "Linda, I am glad I got this job. It is exactly what I wanted."

"You have a great time with your boys this weekend." We started our vehicles at the same time, but she drove off first. As I warmed up the engine I had to secure everything in the camper for travel down the permafrost-heaved roads. I got the box of cassette tapes out and put them in the other front seat, since there was no radio station receivable on many miles of the road. Lastly, I did my safety check on all lights and tires, climbed back up into the driver's seat and started out the dusty parking lot. It felt really good to go.

Once driving, I realized I was going to be very hungry long before I got to Palmer. There was only one fast food place on the 200 plus miles of road home, Tastee Freez in Glennallen. I called on the cell.

"Hi, I'm Linda Thompson. I teach at Kenny Lake School. I am just leaving now and will be at your place in about forty to forty-five minutes. I'm in a hurry. Any chance you could have a burger and a chocolate shake ready for me when I drive up so I won't have to wait?"

"Sure. We'll have it ready to go."

"Thanks a million." I turned the phone off and drove sixty miles an hour, five miles over the speed limit. I knew my chances of being pulled over by an Alaska State Trooper were slim to none at that speed.

The burger and shake were almost ready when I drove up. In five minutes, I was on my way again.

As I drove mile after mile toward home, I anxiously looked forward to a wonderful, loving soft hug from Erik and a scrunching love hug from Chris. I was so excited that I managed to stay awake all the way home. When I did get sleepy, I stuck my head out in the cold wind and let it shock me awake. The bugs were not out in great numbers, but there was always the chance that I would catch a bee or fly between my teeth if I didn't wake up fast.

At 9, Peggy and I drove up at the same time. I jumped out of the van and ran to the car just as the boys jumped out.

"It's good to see you, boys!" We scooped each other up in hugs. Suddenly, it seemed as if I had been gone a lifetime.

"It's great to be home, Mom," said Chris as he walked in the house, carrying the suitcase from Grandma's car.

"Chris, tell your grandma thanks," I said.

"Thanks, Grandma, for letting me stay at the homestead," he said with a smile.

"Thanks, Grandma," said Erik.

"You're welcome, boys." She looked at me. "I'm sure you have a lot to talk about with the boys. We can talk tomorrow."

"Thanks for taking care of them for me. What a week! I love my new job. It's perfect."

We waved goodbye as Grandma drove off. Erik stayed close, hugging me as we walked into the house.

The three of us hung out together in the loft until midnight, lying on the luscious white Berber carpet while looking up at the cathedral ceiling. Erik played with his tracings and books while Chris and I talked about our week apart. I told Chris that he had to go with me on Sunday. He accepted his fate with unhappiness, curiosity, and mischievousness. He knew he would have to push me to get freedom as a teenager but that he had lost this particular battle before it started.

"Okay, Mom. But let's make a deal here. I'll go with you if I can go with my friends to play Dragon Raid tomorrow night. It will be my last night," he said, successfully making me uncertain and worried. Things would be much easier if I had a husband with whom I could discuss what this young man needed, but I didn't have that luxury.

"All right." I didn't like it, but on the other hand, we were moving and there wouldn't be more of these kinds things in Kenny Lake. I was certain of that.

"Come on, boys, bedtime." I turned off the lights, and the three of us went down the stairs to the daylight basement. I sent the boys to bed and I happily took a whirlpool bath. Ahh, it was *great*, especially after those cold showers every morning in the high school locker room. Once we were all in our beds I felt gratitude for being home safe with my boys, happily grounded again.

Chapter Four
Chris

After a weekend of nonstop packing, storing boxes of things I wouldn't need in Kenny Lake, and cleaning, Chris and I started driving back to Kenny Lake with the van completely full. It was Sunday afternoon, and Grandma had already picked up Erik from the house.

"First thing we have to do is find a place to live. The camper in the school parking lot isn't the best hotel," I told Chris.

"What are our options, Mom?"

"I'm still hoping for a warm cabin with an oil stove for heat, a cook stove, and running water. Linda, my aide, said she would help us by calling around for places this weekend.

We drove past Sutton, up and down the hills on narrow winding roads, and past the Matanuska Glacier, until we finally made it to the high-altitude pass at Eureka Summit, where the roads widened before the gas station and restaurant. The road was lined on both sides by tall metal poles with reflectors on them. All the trees were scattered, short, and stubby.

"Snow must really get deep here, Chris, if they feel they need to have markers twenty feet tall along the side of the road."

I looked over at him. He was sound asleep with his head back and his mouth wide open. His book was just about to fall on the floor.

I have always had a problem with falling asleep at the wheel. As soon as I see someone else sleeping in the car when I'm driving, I want to join in and rest. Soon I was struggling to stay awake. I just gave up. Next time I found a pull-off, I took advantage of it. I remembered to turn off the headlights before I climbed to the back of the camper and up to the bed on top. Quickly, I was sound asleep. I don't usually need a long nap. This one lasted about twenty minutes, exactly what I needed to stay awake the rest of the way.

Miles and miles of newly constructed roads were already falling apart from the drastic weather changes from summer highs of ninety degrees to winter lows of sixty below zero. The roads were cracked both perpendicular and horizontal to the direction of the traffic. A person couldn't daydream in conditions like this. Driving was tricky, and though the chance of running into an Alaska State Trooper in the area was pretty slim, we occasionally did find them. We let all the speeders pass us.

Suddenly, there was Mount Drum straight ahead. That was the first indication that we were within forty miles of Glennallen. The giant snow-capped mountain stood guard over Glennallen.

Tastee Freez was closed by the time we made it to town, so we just drove on through to the Richardson Highway and turned right for Kenny Lake.

"We gonna sleep in the parking lot at school, Mom?" Chris asked.

"I don't know where else to go, Chris."

By the time we got there, it was 9 p.m. and getting dark. We parked the van by my classroom door and unloaded all the school supplies that I had hauled from the Palmer house.

"There, now there's enough room for us to use the camper tonight," I said. "Chris, get your toothbrush and use the bathroom in the school before bedtime. I'll park the camper over in those trees. Come on out when you're ready."

We slept all night like babies in the camper. I was exhausted and Chris had no worries. The next day, when Mrs. Tansy drove up, the sound of her car on the gravel was like an alarm clock. I scraped the heavy condensation off the window to see who it was. Brrr, it was cold outside my sleeping bag.

"Hey, Chris, a teacher's here. If we are going to take a shower, we'd better do it now." We got up quickly, grabbed our towels, soap, combs, and clothes and headed for the gym before anyone else arrived. I checked the thermometer outside the office window: +34 degrees.

"Beware, the water in the shower might still be icy."

By the time I got out of my quick, but thankfully warm shower, my day was back to normal. I waited for Chris to dress and connected him with his English teacher, Mrs. VanWyhe. She'd help him get everything together. I ran off to my classroom across the parking lot to make sure my thoughts were in order for school.

The day flew by quickly. During lunch I had a chance to talk to Linda about finding a place to live.

"There are two trailers a mile from the school," said Linda. "You could maybe rent one of them right away. The other one is for sale now. If no one buys it, you can rent it for the winter in October."

"I'm afraid of trailers," I said. "They're such firetraps here in Alaska. I would rather have a log cabin—warmer, too. Chris and I are okay in the camper. I want to find the right place. Erik can stay with Grandma until then. He will need help with bathing, a toilet, and warmth. The camper is too small and too cold for all three of us. Kenny Lake is cold. It is only August and the temperature last night was 34 degrees. Good thing we have twenty-below-zero sleeping bags."

"I know of a cabin at the top of the hill on the Richardson Highway," said Linda. "It could be perfect, but doesn't have running water. Most places don't. Let's go look after school."

"Okay. I'll get Chris right after school, and we can go together. He should be involved. I don't think he is very happy right now and maybe making some decisions with me will help him get through it."

Starting school in Kenny Lake was both exciting and upsetting for Chris. He was happy that his mom finally had the job that she desired, but it wasn't what he wanted. He didn't express his unhappiness in words, but it was easy to tell how he felt by his behavior. The first indication of possible problems occurred when he slept almost all the way from Palmer to Kenny Lake. He never saw the beautiful mountains and breathtaking views as we traveled. Sleep was a way to avoid experiencing the sudden change. I had seen this behavior in children years before in Fairbanks when I worked in a home for girls. They dealt with uncontrollable change in their lives by sleeping it off until they adjusted. I hoped Chris would eventually learn to enjoy what Kenny Lake had to offer.

To add to the frustration he was harboring, I caused major problems on his first day. Linda, Chris, and I jumped in her van after school to look at a place that was possibly for rent. As we pulled off the road, we saw a two-story cabin (about 30 feet X 20 feet) with walls made of three-sided logs. I was so busy looking at the cabin that I shut Chris's van door before he had moved his hand from the door jamb. He screamed in pain. I quickly opened the door and he pulled out a crushed, mangled finger. It instantly started to swell. We had no ice and no instant cure for him at the time. We quickly looked at the cabin since we were already there. Chris walked around, complaining about his hand, shooting angry looks at me. I didn't blame him for being angry. I had been absent-minded and careless.

Peering in the windows, I saw a small oil stove, part of a kitchen counter, and a stairway leading up to the small loft. No furniture and no kitchen stove. Also I had hoped for a place with a shower and indoor toilet.

"I have been trying to get ahold of the owners all weekend to see if they would rent it to you, but they have not returned my calls," Linda said.

I wasn't sure if this place would work. It was seven miles from school, and didn't have everything I thought we needed.

Next to the cabin was a destroyed wellhouse with its insulation spread all outside on the cranberry bushes that surrounded it. The door was ajar. It obviously didn't work.

For the next two days Chris was in a lot of pain. I could tell the bone wasn't broken but he couldn't play his bagpipes because it hurt so badly. We really missed his music, and I heard a lot of, "Why are you doing this to me?" He was more furious than I had ever seen him. I knew I had better tread softly around him for a few days.

Erik, on the other hand, was happily settled in a spare bedroom at Grandma's. We hired a respite worker to help her. At least I didn't have to worry about him. If I could just find a place for us to live, I would enroll him in my special education class. Our living accommodations would have to have a toilet and a way to bathe him. There was no way that he could camp out, like Chris and me, and stay clean for school. It turned out that the cabin where Chris' finger was smashed was not for rent, anyway.

At night, Chris tossed and turned in pain to the point that he actually broke the safety rail in the camper. After that, Chris didn't want to go look at cabins again. Daggers flew from his eyes at the mere mention. Eventually, his entire nail swelled up and was floating high above the finger. We took him to the doctor in Glennallen, and they removed the nail so a new one could grow. That was only the beginning of the complaints. I had opened up Pandora's Box, but didn't know it yet.

Chris met the Wellman boys, Tyler and Travis. Their father was the science teacher, and Chris immediately liked both of them. He left the cabin search and finger smashing up to me and spent his time with his new friends.

The only other log cabin I was able to look at was a little 18 foot X 18 foot one. It had a polluted well and a very small loft. The biggest problem was the shaky, folding pull-down stairs. When the stairs were unfolded, they blocked the tiny living room. Every time Erik wanted to go up, Chris and I would have to help him maneuver them. The stairs were a major obstacle. The cabin wasn't right for us.

I worked every day until bedtime in my classroom, and by the end of the week I had once again not had time to get serious about finding the perfect place to live. By that time Chris was thinking that his mother was totally crazy. How could I have dragged him out to such a terrible place? The kids at school were nice enough to him, but there was nothing to live in, and I had smashed his bagpipe finger. He really missed the luxuries in Palmer. I was in the doghouse with Chris.

Friday, we drove to our beautiful home in Palmer. We could only talk about how wonderful home was. He didn't mention how angry he was with me. I was really having second thoughts by this time. Had I made a serious mistake by taking this job, even though I still loved every minute of the work? It was wonderful to see my days just fly by, unlike when I had been a substitute teacher and every day seemed like an eternity. I was so grateful not to be working in Palmer.

After a wonderful weekend of hot tubs, clean, roomy rooms and packing, Chris and I headed back to Kenny Lake for another week.

At the beginning of week three, a family offered to let us housesit. They were living in Point Barrow for the winter, so we moved into their log cabin. The low-ceilinged, saggy-roofed cabin was very old, filled with wonderful books, and surrounded with hundreds of acres of wilderness. There was a furnace, hot water heater, and water tank under the house, in a dirt crawlspace. I would have to learn how to use the equipment. I would have to haul water in a trailer from the fire hall eight miles away. It seemed intimidating, but I figured I could learn anything.

Two days later, the owners had second thoughts and changed their minds. I was not certain why. Maybe they didn't have confidence in my ability to figure out their water system. Maybe they were afraid we would burn down the place or ruin the old carpeting and old furniture. It was obvious, though, that they loved the cabin and didn't want anyone living in it for the winter. We immediately cleaned it up, cleaner than when we moved into it the day before, and moved back into the camper. We were a little shocked, but thought there was something better in store for us. Where, we knew not.

Chris' finger was mending nicely, and the temperature in the camper continued to drop. By the last day of the week, there was ice on the inside of the windows.

"Ice the first week of September!" I declared that morning. I had been in an early fall only one other time. It was when our family was traveling from the Behnke homestead at Wasilla to Juneau in August of 1984. Chris was two years old. We had left in a rainstorm, and by the time we got to Tok, we were in a major snowstorm. We had no clothes for the weather. In fact, we were wearing summer clothes and sandals. It was one very cold night for the four of us, camping in our little tent somewhere between Tok and the Canadian border.

Chris didn't want to live in the camper with me anymore-more daggers. For the rest of the week, he either slept on the floor of my classroom or at Dave and Gay Wellmans' house on a cot in their living room. Their house was under construction, full of stacks of sheetrock, but was warm, bright, and very friendly. He loved being with his new friends.

I worked hard all week and was getting desperate about getting my family together. I missed Erik terribly. The only place I could find was the green and white doublewide trailer about one mile from school. It looked okay through the windows, but I was still afraid to live in a trailer because of their reputation for being firetraps. It was everything I didn't want but we were running out of time and choices. I rented it by phone Friday night after school, even though I had never walked inside. It was time to get out of the cold.

On weekend four, Chris and I drove to Palmer and packed furniture on a flatbed trailer that we borrowed from a friend, Ted Myers. It took us forever to pack our three beds, dressers, tables, chairs, couch, lounge chair, tool boxes, etc.

As we were working, Erik stood at the side, rocking back and forth.

I said, "Boys, you understand that life isn't going to be so easy, don't you? It'll be colder than Palmer, and there will be wood to split and water to haul."

"It's okay, Mum. I'll help and so will Erik."

"Think of this as an adventure. It'd be a shame to miss it. So far, finding a place to live has certainly been one."

Chapter Five
Cat Trailer

Once everything was wrapped tightly in blue tarps and secured with all the ropes we could find, we put the camper to bed for the winter in the Palmer house garage. Finally, I was going to be grounded with both my boys again. The trailer was only a half-mile from the Wellman's, and Chris was thrilled to be able to hang with his friends every day after school. At least that made him happy for a change! I was quite happy to leave the camper behind, thinking that the new green and white trailer I had rented had to be better because it was much larger. Little did I know what I had done.

We headed down the Glenn Highway to Kenny Lake in the truck. Even without ice on the road, the little six-cylinder Toyota truck had a very hard time pulling the trailer up the steep mountainous roads over the pass. We finally arrived seven hours later at 9 p.m.

I was exhausted, but needed to unload everything before I went to bed. Judging by my previous week's behavior, once school started the next day, I would forget everything about my private life until about 6 p.m. after school. By the lights of the truck, I opened the shed entry door with the key.

As it opened, I was overwhelmed by the smell of mold and mildew, just the things that cause me to sneeze.

"Oh, crud!" I exclaimed.

"What is it, Mom?" Chris asked.

"I think I have rented us a dump. I had no choice!" I whined furiously. "This was all there was!"

The lean-to was built right on the dirt, and the foundation must have been rotting. By the light of the truck headlights, I was able to see the dilapidated lean-to interior with dirty grey indoor/outdoor carpet and 2 inch x 6 inch steps that led up to a bent aluminum door with a broken-out window. I reached around the inside, found a light switch, and flipped it on. I walked up the stairs, grasped the door handle, and had to pull it toward me to walk in. As I pulled, it jammed on the stairs and caught me by surprise in the chest, making me fall back down the stairs. I tried again, being more careful to avoid collision.

"Chris, find the flashlights. Watch out for this broken door. It'll catch you," I called.

Using my flashlight, I quickly walked through the doublewide, and remembered what the superintendent had said to me. I was a bundle of emotion: anger that I had paid $950 to stay in the filthy place, guilt for the boys, and frustration. I ran back outside to the boys.

"Okay, you know how I have always said, 'Always take your shoes off?'" I said.

"Yes, Mom," said Chris and Erik in unison.

"Well, this place is different. My rule here will be. '*never* take your shoes off until you get in your beds at night.' Did you find your flashlights? I can't find any light switches that work except in the kitchen and the bathroom."

Erik sat in the truck, rocking, as Chris and I walked through the place, looking at everything. Chris was sneezing worse than I was. He was a mess. In the kitchen I found all the shelves were full of mouse poop and urine. The floor was covered in it.

"Mom, what is that smell?" Chris asked.

"Smells like mold and cat urine and ah … I think it's fox. It's so dark; I can't really see what the floor looks like. I'm sure tomorrow will be informative." Suddenly, something grabbed my foot, and I fell on the carpet in the den. As my hands hit the greasy carpet, they slid on the slime and caught in long strings of the unraveled flooring. I disentangled my fingers and shined the flashlight on my feet. Several long carpet strings were wrapped around my tennis shoes. I unraveled them, and Chris gave me his hand to help me stand up.

"Pick up your feet as you walk. The carpet is falling apart and all greasy and gucky. Yuck! I don't want to live here, but it's almost winter! We can't live in the icy camper any longer. There's no choice," I whined.

"Maybe we should have stayed in Palmer in our wonderful warm house with no money," Chris said.

"Don't even remind me! I'm an idiot. I signed a contract ... ." We walked back outside to the truck. "Okay, boys, let's pretend we're going camping. We'll pretend until we can find something better."

I sent Chris off to ask the Wellmans to help us. Quickly, they arrived in the dark to assist us. We left headlights on in the vehicles for our safety.

The place stunk overwhelmingly. My left hand kept going up to plug off the assault of the smells. I thought I would vomit but my body adjusted or deadened to the smell within about ten minutes. That urge at least went away, though nothing else did.

The bedrooms, living room, den and hallway were light-less. Some little desk lamps were the last things I had packed in the truck, so I knew exactly where they were. We put them in special places so we could find our way through the dark living room to the bedrooms.

Psychologically, the dark brown walls and dirty, mangy, black carpeting (once orange and beige) were a depressing challenge for us after having lived in a spacious white house with white carpet and generous built-in lighting. I should have never sent the owner the money before I was able to get inside of the place. At least I could have bargained on the rent.

Once I had safety lights on, I called Erik. "Okay, you can come in now." I helped him up the lean-to stairs, past the broken door to the inside. He just stood there and looked for a place to sit down.

"Come on, you need to help us move in. If you are going to go to bed tonight, you have to help. Carry boxes from the truck to the door of the lean-to." I helped him get back outside and showed him his job.

I was grateful to have my family together again, but I tried to not think about living in such a filthy, unsanitary home. That first night, when the broken door threw me down the stairs several times, I swore I would find something else as soon as possible that was cleaner and more to my standards. It was impossible to imagine ever getting that trailer clean without massive carpet removal, paint, and gallons of pure Clorox bleach. If only I could find a log cabin with a plywood floor that I could wash.

I was so grateful to the Wellmans who came that first night to help us get the furniture and boxes in and out of the weather. As crews of people carried things into the house, I directed all sealed boxes to be put in the middle of the living room until daylight. The mattresses, sealed in plastic bags, were left out on the trailer until the bed frames were set up in each bedroom. I didn't want the beds to touch the floor. Everyone had to be extra careful not to fall as they carried things in, because of the stringy carpeting. They all left about 10:30 p.m. I searched for the boxes with sheets and blankets and made all three beds for the night.

Chris was continually sneezing. "Are you coming down with a cold?" I asked.

"Not that I know of, Mom. I was fine until we got here," he said.

I had never seen him sneeze like that before.

The next day we all went to school early in the morning and took hot showers in the locker rooms. I was in a routine by the fourth week. When I walked into the shower room, I immediately turned on the precious water to warm up.

Chris also was in the habit of letting the water run to warm up. He took care of Erik. After checking the water temperature, he made sure his brother used soap and got wet. He turned off the water for Erik and handed him a towel when he was done. Erik just squatted down on the floor of the locker room with the towel on his back like a superman cape. He didn't dry off.

"Mom, I've got to go," Chris called.

"Go ahead. I'll get him. Thanks for helping." I posted a sign in the boys' locker room stating, "Woman Inside" and helped Erik get dry and dressed. I quickly showed Erik around the high school, which was slowly filling with staff and students. I introduced him to Syvie and Mrs. Tansy. Both were really loving and kind to him. Erik apparently felt right at home immediately. He didn't find any need to rock. He stood like the others and tried to make conversation with the adults who were standing around talking. I finished checking my school mail, and the two of us walked over to my classroom to meet Linda and Marlene Roig.

After school that day, Rick Oatman came to my rescue and hauled a load of water for the trailer. The landlord said that the water heater worked great and I trusted her word. We looked forward to showers the next morning.

I unpacked cooking supplies and started to clean the cupboards, but changed my mind. I needed to trap all the mice before there was any point to cleaning. I closed the boxes and set most of them on the kitchen counter. We would use utensils right out of the box. With a pot, knife, and spoon, we cooked a simple dinner of salmon chowder, using powdered milk, home-canned salmon, tomatoes from my greenhouse, potatoes, dill, canned corn and carrots from my garden. At least the mice couldn't get the leftovers in the fridge.

There was an old, rusty, chipped hanging lamp over the dining room area where we had put our table and four chairs. At least there was one place where we could see. We all sat under the light that night, quietly eating together. I looked around the room during dinner and finally accepted my fate—at least for the time being. After we did the dishes, I worked on schoolwork, Chris did tons of homework, and Erik did his beautiful coloring, sitting under the little, broken dining room lamp. Microscopic no-see-um bugs continually attacked us. We were all soon covered with little, red, swelling bites like acne. Even with the frost at night, these bugs continued to thrive in that house the entire time we lived there.

The next morning, Chris hopped into the trailer shower. He turned on the water, but it only sputtered a few drops and quit. What had happened to our water? Was there something I needed to do? I went out in the entry and dropped a dipstick in the tank, only to find that all the water was gone! The water system, like everything else about the place, was in bad need of repair. The 400-gallon tank of water had all leaked out through many holes in the pipes under the trailer.

Somehow, I had to haul more water the next day and start the long process of learning about leaky water systems. I had been told by the owner, when I paid the expensive rent that things worked in this trailer. They didn't. Yes, I had a lot to learn about landlords, bad rentals and water systems.

The first week the temperature dropped each night, and we turned on the furnace. It ran like a squeaking sputtering engine with no lubricant. I worried about it catching the place on fire. It spewed out little heat and a lot of carbon monoxide. I called the owner and complained about everything, but she was totally unsympathetic. She had her rent money and security deposit. The rest seemed to be my problem. The furnace was the only thing she was willing to fix. On the second day we were there, a repairman drove from Glennallen. He worked on the furnace for a couple of hours and soon had it running. The noise from it was incredible. It was good that Erik never complained about anything and Chris couldn't hear very well. The racket never bothered either one of them. The only problem was that every time it went on, blowing air into Chris's room, he sneezed non-stop until long after it finished its cycle. He had never been allergic to anything before.

My bedroom was on the opposite end of the trailer. It was the farthest from the furnace, thus the coldest. It had a window that faced north toward Mount Drum and another that faced the highway to the southeast. I loved the windows in the daytime, but never spent much time in my room because it was so cold. The master bedroom closet doors were the nicest things in the trailer. They were ten feet of mirror with no scratches or damage. I had a place to hang a few things, but mostly kept everything in the boxes stacked up on top of each other. I thought everything would be safe from critters if they were closed up. I was wrong.

Erik's room smelled the most like cat, fox, and urine. I wasn't sure why. As soon as I could, I vacuumed several times in an attempt to remove whatever was in the carpet. It made no difference. The door to his room had been bashed in on the bottom, and someone had put pieces of plywood over the holes. It closed, sort of, so he had some privacy.

The living room opened up to the dining room and the TV room. There was a large wood stove where we put big metal buckets of water to heat. We chopped wood and tried to keep the fire burning all the time, since Chris seemed to sneeze less from the wood fire than from the smelly oil stove that was probably gassing us to death. The room's very large north-facing windows were its one redeeming feature.

Each night, when we returned late from school, all I wanted was to move out. I continued to ask everyone I met if they knew of a cabin we could rent for the winter. I soon realized the "joke" the superintendent had cracked during my interview was actually true. There was absolutely no chance I could find a better place with a well and plumbing. I would definitely have to haul water, no matter where we lived.

During that first week we realized all kinds of problems with this very expensive barnyard. Along with the torn, dirty carpet, the fuel oil smell from the old, rattling furnace; the bashed doors, and broken windows; the one bathroom that no longer worked; and of course the broken front door, the biggest worry for me was that the water system was in a lean-to. There was no heat source. This was one of the coldest parts of Alaska. We could count on many days colder than −20F. The entire water system would freeze before the water ever got into the trailer, so even if we got the leaks fixed, we were in trouble. I wasn't even considering what it would be like when the temperature dropped to −60F in December and January. It was obvious to me that the landlord had no idea or didn't care how absolutely impossible this place was to live in. Did she want me to install a new stove to heat the lean-to? I didn't want to invest a dime more of my money to fix up her mess. Nightly, I prayed for a better place to live. We continued to pretend we were camping. As we thought along those lines, it was somewhat tolerable.

All month, every other day, I hauled water in the back of the truck in thirty-gallon trash cans from the community well. I purchased a little $100 water pump and proceeded to pump water from the truck into a hole in the wall where a pipe led down into the big tank in the lean-to. After about two hours of hauling and pumping, I would have about sixty gallons in the system. I found that if I turned off the valve from the water storage tank, it would stay all night. The next morning, when we wanted to wash dishes or take a sponge bath, we opened the valves for immediate use and quickly closed them to conserve whatever water we could.

Chris was great about helping me for a week or so, but then he lost interest. He would always say, "I'll just take a shower at school." He was ready to disown me as a mom. "All the work of hauling water, and for what?" he said. He couldn't even take a decent shower. As far as he was concerned, it was better in Palmer, even if we were broke all the time. Little Kenny Lake School was much more demanding academically than Palmer High had been. He liked the ease of getting through high school in Palmer and resented all the work that came with a lot of personal attention from the dedicated staff at Kenny Lake.

Each weekend we would drive back to Palmer to get another load of food and other things from the house. We were all so joyful when we walked in the door of our Palmer house on weekends. I loved my new job, but the contrast between the two lifestyles was upsetting, even for me. We would kick off our shoes, enter in our clean socks, and lie on the plush white carpet to look up at the beautiful cathedral ceiling, at all the exposed wood beams and beautiful woodwork I had carefully designed when the house was built. Even with the mess from packing, it seemed immaculate. We missed our home, but that was all I missed.

Every Sunday, we dragged our feet and left at the last possible moment to head back to Kenny Lake. If it hadn't been for the amazing things that were already unfolding with Erik's education, I wonder if I would have completed my contract for the year. Little did I know exactly how unhappy Chris was at this time and the possibility of him leaving us.

For one month we lived under these horrible conditions, never unpacking. We camped out, cooking one-pot meals, using paper plates, spending long days at school, and nights sitting high on chairs under the one dining room light, and climbing into our beds in the dark rooms just to get up early to rush to school and take showers in the high school gym before staff and students arrived. Chris continually tried to instruct Erik on bathing. I would relieve him when he tired of the responsibility. It was a lot to ask of him, but he did it and was a wonderful brother to Erik.

Everything was still in boxes when on October 8 we heard that we could rent another trailer across the highway. It was half the size, looked brighter, and had ceiling lights in the rooms. I heard from Mr. Friendshu, a math teacher, who had been a former renter, that the plumbing system had been fixed to work year 'round. The owners were an honest Christian family who lived in Kenny Lake, and would maintain it. We didn't have to suffer any longer in the big moldy cat trailer. As soon as possible that day, I booked a viewing of the second trailer, made a deal with the owner and paid rent for the month.

The Kenny Lake hockey team came after school to help us move. In less than two hours, our furniture and boxes were across the street, piled in a big heap in the middle of the living room.

By 10 p.m. Gay Wellman and I had finished vacuuming the tattered cat house trailer carpet, cleaning the sinks and counters and mopping the vinyl kitchen floor. I was exhausted when I locked the door happily and drove across the highway to trailer number two.

Chapter Six
Erik Starts School

We found Linda hard at work on Erik's first day of school when we arrived in the morning.

"Linda, this is Erik, my older son," I said.

"Nice to meet you, Erik. Welcome to our school," Linda said.

Erik smiled and said, "Yes." Then he spotted his books and walked over to the little classroom library.

Linda looked at me with a quizzical but understanding look. She realized that he had not understood what she had said.

"Erik, would you like to do art in school?" I asked him.

"Oh yeah, yeah," he whispered with a smile on his face.

"I have been thinking about you making cards. If you do a good job, we could print them and you could sell them to gift stores."

Erik stopped looking at the books and gave me a big smile. I wasn't sure if he understood me, but he did like the idea of getting to do art in school. His eyes focused on me. "Fun," he said.

"Linda is going to work with you on this. I will be able to help more after school."

During the first day, Linda was experimenting with Erik. She put a Xerox copy of an outline of a duck in front of him to color. She didn't expect much. But no one expected much out of him. At the end she showed me the beautifully colored page. She wanted to believe in him but she was conditioned, just like I was, to only see the limitations.

I said, "It's nice, but not marketable. We can't sell someone else's black-line drawing. That's someone else's duck."

"I guess you're right. He sure can color though," said Linda.

Almost every day after school, the three of us would meet to discuss the art of the day. After the school buses were loaded, I would go to Erik's desk with great anticipation. Linda would be bubbly, and I would be the critic.

The next day she tried how-to art books that taught drawing. Erik drew pictures almost identical to the ones in the books only smaller. The problem was that they looked like they were traced. Erik clearly had the ability to produce an accurate, proportional copy of practically any drawing put before him, but they were still just copies of someone else's ideas.

"Erik, these sports pictures are very cute. I looked at Linda. "What did he draw them from?"

Erik showed me a how-to-draw book with a baseball player and a hockey goalie, very similar to his own.

"These are really great. Problem is they are still not marketable. That's the goal here. He needs to do his own thing, not what some author or art teacher says he should do. If Erik is to design cards, they have to be his style."

What could he do with photos? Linda and I wondered. "Erik, how about wildlife? You've seen plenty of caribou, whales, moose, bear, and tons of fish. You certainly know what they look like in the wild," I said.

Erik looked at me, but didn't respond.

"Erik, let's try drawing animals. Okay?"

"Sure," he said with confidence.

Linda got excited about the new plan. Even though school was out, and her husband Charlie needed his dinner cooked, she grabbed Erik's hand. "Erik, let's go to the public library and find some pictures for ideas." By this time, Erik adored Linda and would follow her anywhere. She was always praising him, telling him how wonderful his art was. The two bundled up in their parkas and headed off in a rainy snowstorm across the parking lot to the Kenny Lake Public Library.

The wonderful thing about Linda was she loved Erik. She really wanted this project to work and was dedicated like no one had ever been before. It was her dedication and perseverance that led to the first breakthrough.

Little by little Linda grew to trust Erik's artistic talent. She realized that he already had the skills he needed. Instead of acting like a regular art teacher and encouraging him to do a certain specific kind of art, we needed to give him the creative room to develop and do his own thing. We had no idea what that might be. Old wildlife books helped us narrow our plans down to the possibility of Alaskan animals, a subject that would certainly be marketable during the tourist season. Linda knew where the best thick, white drawing paper was stored at school, and she soon purchased Erik's first UniBall Vision fine black ballpoint pen from Glennallen. (He still prefers this pen, nine years later.) There weren't a lot of books compared to Anchorage libraries, but there were enough.

The end of that first day, when we encouraged him to draw animals, I sat typing IEP data sheets and gathering ideas for the next day's classes when Linda came into the portable classroom. As always, the furnace was making a racket and she said loudly. "Did you see these?" She was very excited, almost to the stage of bubbling over. She took some sheets out of a secret folder on her seemingly disorganized little desk.

The black ink drawings were unrefined but interesting. I saw them as childlike images, certainly not anything marketable yet. I wasn't sure if I should be impressed. That was the difference between Linda and me at this point. She saw the potential in those first freehand drawings. I only saw what I had seen all of Erik's life. In my mind, he still had no future, but in my heart I prayed we were right about there being something. I wasn't going to give up hope, not yet anyway. We'd just started this project.

The next week, I was hunting for a particular book. Linda and Erik huddled over his desk together, working on one of his drawings.

"Come look at this," Linda called. "There's something special happening here."

I gathered my papers and books. "Whatcha got, Erik?" I looked at the picture. Even though it was upside down, I could easily see it was an adorable eagle. I was amazed. I couldn't believe that he had drawn it. "Did you draw this, Linda? It looks like a copy."

"No, Erik did."

"I bet he was dying to color it," I said.

"Oh, yeah. I had to snatch the black-line drawing and Xerox it right away so he had something to color. I didn't want him to ruin the original until we figured out what to do next. He was pretty upset with me but getting to color the copy finally calmed him down."

"You didn't draw it?" I said. "Then where did he get the idea?" She showed me a photograph of an eagle in a tree at Mt. McKinley Park.

His drawing was nothing like the original, and yet it was clearly a bald eagle. I compared the original photo to the drawing.

"You didn't trace it, Erik. Your image is too large. It's a very different look from the original. Wonderful! Sure you didn't draw it, Linda?" I questioned.

"I sure didn't. It's all his work," she said.

"Wow! Do you suppose he can do more of these? I want to believe what I see, but I am afraid that my hopes will be crushed. Did you hear me, I have hope! Could this be a fluke?" Linda and I watched Erik quietly work adding color to his reproduced drawing.

"We'll see, won't we? I don't think it is. It is amazing, that's for sure," said Linda.

I walked over to the window by my desk several minutes later and looked out at the happy little chickadees on a spruce tree outside. A sense of peace surrounded me. "God, is this the reason we are in Kenny Lake?" We needed to discover that Erik was more than any of us imagined. He was *gifted*. How had we missed it? It had been there, but no one had dreamed big enough. Even Erik hadn't. Suddenly it was clear why I could never get a job in Palmer. The right people weren't there. The team he needed was in Kenny Lake.

Linda loved everything he did, and the praise was like a thick fog in the classroom. Erik was very patient with us both as we figured him out. I didn't have time to help as much as I wanted during the school day. I would look over his shoulder whenever I could, and give suggestions to help him, if Linda was off teaching speech to someone else. I continued to critique his work at the end of each day, just like I did all of my special education students' assignments. I was a tough critic. After all, I had twenty years of limiting ideas in my background. I had dreams, but they were hammered down into the back of my mind by my former limiting, negative experiences. If he was to be an artist, he would have to do quality work. If I wouldn't buy it, no one else would, was my philosophy. One eagle was great, but Erik was going to have to draw a lot more than that for me to be a true believer in the possibility of a professional art career.

Chapter Seven
Trailer Trapping

Snow fell the week after we moved into the small trailer. I was so glad we had moved. The furnace worked well, and there was a big 500-gallon water tank in an insulated entry room that would never freeze.

There was a large wood stove in the living room. It was wonderful to have a warm place to sit. It reminded me of hot summer nights in Garden Grove, California, sitting outside on the porch with my parents. When the sun shone in Kenny Lake, I loved the feel of the rays of light as they lightly warmed my face, when they came through the window.

The floor sagged in places and the vinyl was split in a lot of places, but at least it had been repaired with a staple gun, so we didn't trip on it. I could go through the entire place (if the boys picked up their things) with a vacuum in fifteen minutes. Mopping took only three more. There were advantages.

The trailer was not up to my standards, but I was living better than a lot of the poor people who lived in that area of Alaska. It was an immense step up from the doublewide trailer across the street. We were grateful to be warm, and able to take showers so easily.

The worst part was the mice. It was that time of year when all the little animals in Alaska madly hunt for shelter from the cold. (Humans weren't the only ones with this problem.) Mice had actually moved into our boxes while we were in the cat trailer but we didn't know it until we went to unpack in the second trailer and I found mouse sign everywhere. It was all fresh, so I knew they were abundant. I "opened up business" just like when I trapped muskrat and beaver in the past. I could handle the numbers. I bought a dozen traps and set them all along the trails through the house. Everyone at school was doing the same. One family lived in a big, new house, and even they were fighting the mouse movement.

One Sunday, after Chris and I had finished reading our church service, I was really cold and set the heater full blast. Erik had left to get his toys. Chris was getting ready to practice his bag pipes. I was all cuddled up under an afghan, and reading the Bible when I felt something crawling up my leg. This was no bug; it was huge. I threw off the afghan. A cute fluffy, brown mouse with big black eyes, stared up at me while hanging off my leg. Little white mouse lice crawled all over his body.

"Chris! Mouse crawling up my leg!" I tried to shake it off. The critter fell off and ran as fast as possible into the kitchen.

Chris came running in with a can in his hand and slammed it down over the mouse so fast that the mouse didn't know what hit him. "Got him, Mom," Chris said proudly.

We eventually were able to slide a piece of cardboard underneath and carry him outside. We let him go close to the highway.

"There you go, little mouse. We aren't taking tenants now. You go find a new nest, not in our trailer." He scampered off in the brush under the spruce and willow trees.

We caught lots of mice the traditional way, but they seemed to get smarter with time. I got tired of the bloodstains and the clean-up after each successful trapping. One day, I discovered mouse sign inside a potato chip bag that had missed the trash can when the boys had thrown it that direction. I had a brainstorm. The next time we drove to Palmer to pick up another load of stuff from our big house, we bought a big box with 36 individual packages of chips.

"Eat all you want, boys," I said.

When we got home, I set a couple of traps and sat at the kitchen table to eat more.

"Eat, eat, boys," I encouraged them. "We have lots to catch."

"Mom, now I see there are advantages to living in a dump—all the chips you ever wanted," Chris said, smiling.

Once six bags were empty, Chris and I started setting other traps around. We'd barely started when we heard a trap snap in the bathroom. I ran down the hall and found the chip bag with a plump little mouse half in and half out of the bag. I picked it up and returned to the kitchen to show off.

"Gets'em every time," I said with a smile on my face. I walked over to the trash can, unhooked the dead mouse, and dropped mouse and bag into the can. Then I set the trap in another newly emptied chip bag.

"I always was a good trapper," I bragged.

I had always tried to have nutritious meals for my boys. Chips were a fattening luxury item, especially in Palmer when we had been watching every penny. We set all twelve mousetraps in the individual chip bags. The grease scent alone was enough to attract the mice inside. An added bonus to this method was that there was no mess. All the blood and yuck were all in the bag. It was cold enough that any remaining mice and shrews hibernated elsewhere and stopped coming. Soon we were fatter around our middles and the house mouse population was conquered.

Early art by Erik David Behnke

Chapter Eight
The Beginning

Linda had days she trusted Erik as an artist and days she didn't. She gathered cartoons, sketches of dragons, and dinosaurs from the library. Erik could draw them accurately, but I couldn't allow that. He needed photographs, real images that he would interpret his own way. The photos simply gave him ideas from which to branch off. Most of the time, there was barely a resemblance to the original photo. The image he produced was clearly his own. He definitely looked at photographic images in a different way than most people.

Early on we realized that all the pens we had were terrible, and our best drawing paper was poor quality, but we didn't let that slow him down. We continued to throw everything we could find at him to draw. We obviously didn't really know what we were doing, but we trusted that we would eventually figure it all out.

In my room, Erik sat with two other students who he really liked, Cassie and Patrick. They were his peers and best friends. Though both of these students were far ahead of Erik academically, they were always nice to him and interested in whatever he had to say, even though it was very difficult to understand him. They both appreciated him for the way he was. They never belittled him or put him down. I learned to truly love these two thoughtful students in Kenny Lake High.

I needed a full-time aide for Erik and other students at school. Linda and I were stretched to the maximum between the two schools. Erik was getting served in some ways and not in others. One goal specified in his IEP was to work in the community but neither one of us had time to arrange it. There were showering goals, but no one to help him. Mr. Carlson, the principal, tried to fill the gap, but it was impossible.

I had been trying to persuade the school district to hire another teacher aide to work just with Erik. He was by far the most disabled student at the school, and needed complete assistance to succeed. Linda couldn't stay with him all day. She had many other speech students. I had twelve other grades of students to teach. Neither of us could give Erik the constant attention he needed. The district was dragging its feet. I had seen it before, many times. Hiring teacher aides for students is a long process. The teacher has to justify the need with many written and oral reports to the principal, the special ed. director, school board, and school superintendent. I was preparing the reports, but I felt I was given the runaround. Eventually, Erik's aide was hired. Even though Erik started school in September, he didn't get an aide, Kim Gregory, until November. This delay is common. Everything takes too long in school districts.

The national trend now in education is to integrate children like Erik into the regular classroom. The regular teacher is assigned too many students to be able to teach everyone at the correct level; thus "generalized goals" for successful integration into society are the focus in many schools at every grade level. I feel it is a "Dump and Run" stage our country is cycling through. Some parents and professionals think it's the way to go, but I disagree emphatically. If I had just dumped Erik in a regular art class, even with an aide, very little would have happened. If Erik had no interest in what was being taught, he would simply tune out. I am not criticizing the dedicated teachers, who try their hardest to accommodate the needs of our special children; I am criticizing the system that thinks one approach works for everyone. It doesn't. Time will show that students like Erik will have social skills, but not necessarily the ability to read, write, do math, or succeed in the work force. We must teach and train people with disabilities to be the best they can be, or we will be creating a welfare society with no chance of individual financial independence.

Erik was often surrounded by all kinds of exciting things to learn and experience in the mainstream, but he didn't reach out to grab the new ideas. He didn't understand them. The class would move onto the next topic the next day, and it was one continual merry-go-round ride of frustration for him. Fortunately, he didn't act angry or disturbed with it. He obediently went to class as scheduled and sat, either watching the class and teacher or rocking, his mind a thousand miles away.

For him to succeed, the focus had to be only on Erik, not on a viable lesson plan. He might have social skills, but not a career. I wanted a career, a successful one, not a minimum one. Just like parents of "normal" children, I wanted Erik to be all that he could be. Mainstreaming, integration, whatever you called it, wasn't enough. Thank goodness I was given the chance at Kenny Lake School in 1997 to give him everything he needed for success.

I had found that it took at least a half a year, and sometimes a whole year, for a new teacher to figure out the special students they had been assigned. Oh, we could jump right in and start the school year fairly effectively in August, but we didn't really understand how each special student learned, what motivated them, and how to teach them, without getting to know them. In Erik's case, we had moved around so much that the teachers rarely were able to move beyond the stage of observing Erik, teaching him by trial and error, trying to figure out his learning style. If we had stayed in the same place, teachers would have moved in and out of his life anyway, as the district reassigned them to new jobs.

Being Erik's parent gave me the advantage. I had a personal investment in him, and I knew him, so I didn't waste any time at the beginning of the school year. It helped too that we didn't go home at a reasonable hour. It was to his benefit to stay and hang out in my classroom as I graded papers, worked on IEPs, cleaned, did record keeping, etc. At the beginning, he did what he wanted: read books and drew pictures after the last bus left. By October, we had figured out how to help him. Since we had so many students, not much was accomplished during his school day. But after school, when we were alone, I could make sure his projects were completed, as I completed my own. (Since he often worked from 7:30 a.m. to 7 p.m. it was not surprising that his career developed so quickly.)

Linda managed to get some interesting black-line drawings out of Erik in October. She really became a believer at that time. When asked later (February 1999) on Channel 2 KTUU TV when the breakthrough came, she said, "I put a photograph of an eagle in front of him and he created this beautiful eagle. I knew that something special was happening here. I was just moved."

He also created "Walking Caribou" and "Flying Goose" which are still my favorites from those early weeks. I was becoming more and more interested and impressed, but still didn't think there was anything marketable. The materials he was using were such poor quality, but I didn't realize that. I just knew I wouldn't buy his art in this form.

The Talon, Kenny Lake School's newspaper, sent student Adam Lain to write an article about Erik for the October issue. This was less than one month after Erik started school. It now amazes me to see what we were planning so early on.

> Erik Behnke, a student at Kenny Lake School, is going into the art business. Erik is transitioning into the work force and hopes to use his artistic ability as a career. He is making original greeting cards from his artwork, which will be professionally printed and marketed statewide. Eventually, Erik hopes to market his work on a home page on the Internet. To develop his business, he will also hold art shows and develop a portfolio of his artwork.

Linda and I were definitely in a dream world when the student reporter arrived for that interview.

The weekly, sometimes daily, dreaming started in October with Linda and me brainstorming. What a team! The ideas came faster than I could write them down. We were like the two good fairies in Disney's *Sleeping Beauty*, fighting over what color Aurora's dress and birthday cake should be. I was sure that ideas were shooting out the walls of the ancient old classroom building in flashes of pink and blue over and over.

The discussions and dreams that these brainstorming sessions prompted were outrageous and we knew it. Erik had just started drawing independently in September, and in October we were writing Individual Education Plan goals and objectives such as:

> 1. Erik will produce pen-and-ink note cards, calendars, and other marketable products on a daily basis.
> 2. Erik will develop at least two methods/ways of packaging his art for consumer accessibility by year's end.
> 3. Erik will promote his product using a least one advertisement method. Erik will have explored other ways to sell his note cards outside the confines of Kenny Lake.

That was a ridiculous, ludicrous dream. Very few people could understand him. How could he develop, package, advertise, and sell a marketable art product? He was drawing a few pictures, but most were not very realistic. We were two dedicated women who wanted nothing less than success for this young twenty-year-old man. We fell in love with a dream, maybe an illusion.

But teaching in this little school had great advantages. I was able to create any course of instruction I wanted, as long as it was in the budget and followed the Individual Education Plan.

For days Linda and I gathered ideas for goals. We wrote them on scraps of paper. Of course, we were always losing them if they didn't make it immediately into a special idea file. Finally, the day came for the scheduled IEP meeting. Linda and I had taught all day and were quickly gathering all our ideas on one pad of paper.

"Okay, I think I have everything. Is there anything else we want to add?" I asked.

"Think that's it," Linda said.

The three of us rushed out the door.

Erik's IEP was the work of four people: Erik, Linda, Reed, and me. Reed did the role of district representative/ special education teacher and put the IEP together. Linda and I fed the process with goals and objectives. Reed had the power to tame down or nix any outrageously expensive goals. Erik rocked. When asked questions, he always answered, "Oh yes, yes." It was a good thing we had his best interests in mind, since he rarely understood what we were talking about.

Linda and I knew the art goals were outrageous. Just in case our dreams didn't come true, we backed up everything with realistic down-to-earth goals. Reed Carlson made sure to protect Erik's education by adding practical goals like working in a grocery store in Glennallen, and by putting in functional self-help living skills, like taking a shower and shaving independently.

When he proposed the grocery store job, I objected. "But we want to focus his year on art, not working in a grocery store."

"I worked in a store when I was young. I learned valuable work skills," he said in justification of the work goals. "I think it would help him. Certainly wouldn't hurt him."

It made sense when he put it that way. Personally, I thought the grocery store was a waste of time since it took an hour to drive to town, but in the end, the goal of working in a grocery store actually accomplished three other extra blessings that helped him, our family, and the school. I would write up lists and he would go shop for the items and pay for our groceries using the "dollar more" concept.

Erik didn't understand change. There was little chance that he would ever understand it if he never got to practice. He could understand that if something cost $3.54 he should give the cashier $4. At least that way, if the cashier made a mistake, or someone wanted to take advantage of him, he would be out less than one dollar.

Once winter set in, we needed fresh food each week. I wouldn't want to drive the long drive to town so having Erik shop for us was wonderful. I never would have asked for this luxury in an IEP. Linda or Kim was assigned to do the weekly excursions in the school van, which also helped out Little Kenny Lake School. Erik picked up the mail from the school district office, across the street from the grocery store in Glennallen. So Reed's grocery store goal ended up being a blessing for all.

The first time Erik's art was shown was at a Copper River School District board meeting November 1997, in Glennallen. Linda and I volunteered to take all the art from Kenny Lake School and set up a display. We took Erik's early Xeroxed black-lines, which he had colored. We glued them onto black construction paper, and hung them up in Glennallen High for the meeting. Lots of people were attracted to them. I sat in the audience before and during the meeting just to watch the response. Many people liked what they saw.

Before the board meeting, parents, teachers, and school board members all walked around the room and looked at the display that Linda and I had set up. Since there were no junior or senior high art classes, everything was from the elementary school or was Erik's. The comments were wonderful. I was the proud parent, and Linda told everyone about Erik and his wonderful artistic ability.

At break in the middle of the meeting, Mary Oden, a young, enthusiastic blonde, the Glennallen High art teacher, approached me. "I love Erik's art. You know, he has a great deal of talent. I think he has real potential."

I just stood there smiling, totally enjoying someone seeing that Erik had potential. At the same time, I wondered if she was exaggerating. I only knew that I loved his work more each day. But was that enough to make it great?

"Have you heard of the National Art Council?" she asked. "Erik needs to go to their meeting next spring."

"No, I haven't," I said.

"It's the national version of the Alaska State Arts Council. I am going to the spring conference. You want to go with me? It'd be wonderful for Erik."

I had never heard of it. I was still wondering if he had talent above personal satisfaction and recreation. Here was a young woman giving me even more hope for his future, though, still overwhelmed with the job at Kenny Lake School, I couldn't see that a wonderful future was possible. How could I fit a trip to some national conference or council meeting into my life? I was having trouble just keeping up with school work, splitting wood, hauling water, and helping

Erik with his art in my classroom. As it turned out, I saw that woman only one other time after that day. She left the district before spring, but still gave me that early hope I so badly needed.

One board member wanted to know more about the artist who had drawn all the animals.

I said, "Oh, that's Erik. He's right here." I turned around intending to gracefully point out his location in the audience.

Erik had slipped out of the seat and was sitting on the carpeted floor. His hands were on his knees; and he was rocking quickly, back and forth. Expressions chased each other across his face as he daydreamed some private adventure.

"Oh, excuse me," I said. I went over to his side and put my hand on his shoulder to stop all the movement.

Once he stopped, he glanced at me with a look that said, "Oh, yes, you want me?"

"Stand up, Erik. I want to introduce you to someone." He stood up, walked up to the board member with me, and actually looked at her directly.

"Erik, I love your art. Keep it up," she said. "I want to see more in the future."

Once again, I was fascinated that people were impressed with Erik's work. I thought it was a fine show for elementary school, but certainly nothing remarkable at the high school level. Mary Oden's comments were very interesting and had gotten my attention. The comment from the unknown school board member was interesting too, but for all I knew, she was no more educated about art than I. Maybe she was just trying to be nice. Being on a board was only a sign that she was a good politician, not an art critic. I was hopeful, and doubtful, simultaneously.

Linda Rutledge and Erik standing by the hockey rink outside our classroom at Kenny Lake School.

Erik on the Glenn Highway during one of our driving breaks.

Kenny Lake Elementary School and the Hawk Building in 1997-9 where most of my special education classes were held. The buildings were sold when the school was redesigned in 2000.

This is how we hauled water. The tank could only be filled half full. When our truck tires were bulging badly from the weight of 2000 pounds of water, we would drive home, quickly pump the water in the house and go get another 250 gallons before the water would freeze in the tank.

The filthy cat/mouse trailer that looked fine on the outside but was a disaster on the inside. I eventually ended up purchasing it and remodeling it the second year we lived in Kenny Lake.

Chapter Nine
Family, Art, and School

Next weekend Erik and I drove to Anchorage to investigate Blaine's Art Supplies. Erik bought only ten Tria marker pens because they were so expensive. They were the best professional markers that we could buy. When we got back to Kenny Lake we handed in the receipt and paid him back with money he had earned selling ice cream at school lunches. Part of his vocational training was to learn to deal with money. The pens stayed in school in Linda's metal candy box.

The next week, I critiqued the art as usual with Erik and Linda. "Did Erik trace this camel?" I asked.

"No, he liked the picture of the camel in this magazine and decided to draw his own," said Linda.

I compared it with the photo, and realized that he had turned the photo into his own version of a camel. He had captured the essence of the animal but had changed it to a more charming version. This was the first work of Erik's that I wanted to frame. It was the "Great Aha" or "Oh My Gosh, My Son Is Really Talented" moment.

The next two weeks, he drew the Brown Owl, the Grey Owl, as well as the Brown Bear that eventually became his business logo. I absolutely loved them. Suddenly I was a true believer. With the new pens, the art came alive. The camel popped off of the page after he added color. I was so excited; I had trouble concentrating during the work day. More and more I found myself walking over to Erik's side to sneak a peek at whatever art he was creating.

Now that color problems were on the way to being conquered, we needed to solve other the technical problems that had been put aside. Erik always used permanent ink, never pencil, to make his black-line drawings. It was inevitable that he would sometimes smear the white paper. The drawings needed to be scanned, so they could be cleaned up using a computer program. I'd been hoping I could push this job off on one of the aides, but they didn't have the time or the skills to handle it. It was going to take someone who could work after school. Both Linda and Marlene had husbands, who wanted their dinner and attentive companionship. I only had two boys. They also wanted their dinner, but they didn't complain as loudly as a husband.

Eventually, I faced reality. Somehow I would have to learn to—I didn't even know what it was I needed to learn. Chris talked me into going to the computer lab at the high school so the high school boys could teach me how to scan Erik's drawings, clean them up, and print them on high-quality paper, thereby getting the best quality black-line possible, far better than we had been producing on the scratchy old copy machine in our classroom.

Chris's friend, Tyler, showed me how one day after school. I'm usually a quick learner and thought I had mastered it after one demonstration. Once Tyler walked away, however, I quickly became confused. One time I would get a perfect print, and the next time it would be off-center, or the wrong size, and a foot or an ear or some other part would be missing. Some just disappeared. Once I saved them, I couldn't find them again. It took me two hours to get just a couple of correct copies. I wondered whether it was worth all the effort.

Three hours of fiddling after school one night, with Erik and me both starving, I gave up, frustrated. Erik and I packed up our things and quickly drove home.

I found Chris on the couch near the wood stove. The house smelled of hot dogs.

"I'm home. I'll have dinner on the table in twenty minutes," I said.

Chris didn't say anything. He was involved in a book.

I quickly whipped together a meal of salmon, stewed tomatoes, and macaroni and cheese, a one pot meal that only took only minutes to fix when we were starving. This was the time for such a creation.

"Okay, dinner's on the table," I called.

Erik immediately was at my side ready to sit down at the table and be served. "Get some bowls and silverware, Erik. Chris, please get some milk."

"I'm not hungry," he said.

"What do you mean, you're not hungry? It is 8 o'clock!. You must be."

"I went home with Travis Wellman and we raided his fridge and cupboards. Then I came home and ate hot dogs until you got here."

"How many did you eat?"

"I don't know. Maybe five or six."

"Chris, I know I don't make your dinner exactly when you want it, but the least you could do is wait until we get home. It would be very thoughtful if you cooked dinner. You can read a cookbook as well as I can. You know I have to work, and we're really on to something with Erik's art. I can't always pop home to cook your dinner. How about if you cook some during the week? We'd certainly appreciate it."

Erik and I ate dinner while our tall, lean Chris continued to lie on the couch and burp after his hot dog dinner. I needed to solve this problem, but how? I could spread myself only so thin. I needed Chris to take up a little of the responsibility for this family. Was I asking too much from this fifteen-year-old? He was physically larger than I was. I had read about responsible inner-city boys helping their single mothers with things like this. Now that we're all older, I realize I expected quite a lot of my self-centered teen, but he was so mature in comparison to Erik. I overestimated his capacity to take on adult responsibilities.

I tried to be a good mother. I always made sure the boys had breakfast. It wasn't fancy, but there was plenty of nutritious food if they wanted to take the time to eat. Chris often skipped it to sleep in. Erik and I ate.

Lunch was Kenny Lake School style. When the bell rang, everyone grabbed their lunches and charged to the gym area. There was no hot lunch program. The forty-five junior and senior high school students brought bags of microwave food from home or bought it from Mrs. Moore's sixth grade class at lunch. It felt like one big family. Students pulled out the three microwaves stored in the home economics kitchen. Four to six students soon crowded around each oven. Four quick lunch meals of mini pizzas, Pizza Pockets, burritos, etc., were placed in each oven with the minutes set at 999 on high. Each student would monitor his own lunch as the food went around and around on the carousel until the food started to overflow its wrappers. When a student grabbed his or her lunch out, someone else would pop in more, slam the door, and punch Start.

A folding lunch table with benches was set up each day in the home ec. room off the gym. The students helped Erik cook his lunch. He was like a younger child to them. They took turns watching out for him and made sure things didn't get too burned. Most of the kids sat around the table and ate together like a big family, chatting of things of interest. After having substituted for four years in the larger schools where I heard so many negative comments, here was a school full of students who watched out for each other.

Chris also liked this sociable time, hanging around the microwave, chatting with everyone. He smiled a lot and laughed, which made me happy. I knew he wanted his distance from Mom, so I tried to give it to him. On the other hand, I always hung around the gym at lunch to make sure things went okay for Erik, and another high school student of mine who needed extra help and supervision. Life at this school was like no other. All students became my children. I sat on the gym floor just like the kids, enjoying it all.

After everyone had eaten, out came the balls. Everyone played catch, basketball, volleyball, badminton, or ping pong. Some of the hockey boys would work out on the weight machines in the corner to bulk up for their combat sport. It was a normal high school with groups of jocks, geeks (Chris, and his friends, Newly, Tyler, and Robert), lovers, etc., hanging out together in their groups.

About halfway through lunch, Reed Carlson, principal, walked in to play basketball with any interested students. He was a tall, thin man with tons of energy. He laughed and played like one of the kids, dashing from one side of the court to the other, and shooting like lightning. The students never felt intimidated on the court by this principal and treated him as an equal when playing.

While the games went on, Erik, Cassie, and I would get boxes of ice cream out of the freezer. With the ice cream in a cooler, we sat down on the sidelines.

"Ice cream, ice cream for sale," I'd call. Students who had money came over immediately to check out what was in the box. They would pick a bar and hand Erik or Cassie a dollar. Whatever didn't sell went back in the freezer in a few minutes, and the money was deposited in the school safe.

Chris came over and sat down with us, something he rarely did at lunch. When sales dropped off he asked, "What happens to all the money, Mom?"

"It will be used to buy art supplies for the classroom. Erik's pens alone cost $13 a color," I said.

"I was wondering, are you gonna start another Special Olympics ski team, Mom? You always do," Chris asked. "You could use the money for that too."

"Erik wants to. Will you help me?" I asked.

"Sure, I'll coach, but I'd rather hang with my friends."

"Okay, I'll see if I can get other volunteers."

"Maybe Linda would help," Chris said.

"I'll ask her. Erik, looks like the bell is just about to ring. Let's get this ice cream put away and head back." The three of us headed across the parking lot with our parkas, gloves, hats and snow boots on, for it was a normal thirty below.

I had everything I wanted. My children were happy, we all had friends who liked us, and people were wonderfully nice to Erik. The only thing I puzzled about was the rumors. I kept hearing that all new teachers at Kenny Lake School were always RIF'ed (reduction in force). *Would they let me go at the end of the year? No, I worked too hard for that.*

Chapter Ten
Building and Growing

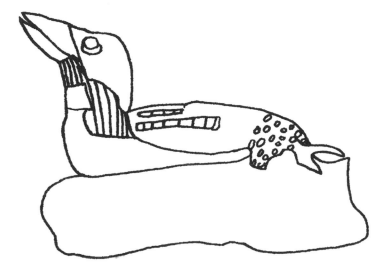

It was obvious that we were being led to everything we needed. I honestly felt God was at our side as we searched for direction. When we'd reach a dead end, sure enough, a new door would open and we would start down a new pathway, guided to what we needed to know about the art profession.

After two or three weeks of nightly frustration, trying to figure out how to scan Erik's art as Tyler had taught me, only to become more and more frustrated, I finally gave in and begged for another lesson. He and Newly most graciously started over and gave me the same lesson again. I had missed one simple rule at the beginning about adjusting the size of what I was scanning. Once I knew how to focus the program on exactly what I needed to scan, all my problems went away. Suddenly, I was in business, and Erik and I didn't waste any more time or paper. I was able to keep up with Erik's black-line output by working just two or three evenings per week, so dinner was served at least a little earlier each night, much to Chris's satisfaction.

The second time Erik's art was displayed was at the Alaska's Down's Syndrome Congress Dinner on November 13 at the Catholic

Church in Anchorage. I walked in and found a roomful of parents just like me. There were children like Erik and Chris of all ages running around cheerfully. I showed the pictures I'd brought to the president of the group. She encouraged me to set up a little display during dinner. I didn't have any way to hang them, so I set out the crude art from the school board meeting and the newly scanned and colored pieces on one of the tables. Many people at the meeting were enthralled with what they saw, even though things were still in the experimental stage. A few were done with the new pens, but most weren't.

A nice-looking man from the Douglas Indian Association (Southeast Alaska) introduced himself. He loved Erik's art, even though it was still rough. He gave me his business card, wrote his home address and phone number, and on the bottom wrote "contact for Rie Munoz." I couldn't believe it.

He said, "Just remember my Samuel," and he introduced me to his little two-year-old boy who also had Down's. Erik had to succeed, not only for himself, but for other children like Samuel and for the parents like Samuel's father. Now I saw that Erik gave parents hope.

This must be where we need to go next for guidance. I was so thrilled I could hardly contain myself. It was my first connection with the art world. Rie Munoz was my idol. I loved her art. She was famous in the Northwest. We would try to make contact with her over Christmas when Erik went down to visit his father. Maybe she could help.

———◆———

Linda introduced Erik to any and every kind of picture she loved. He drew lots of black-lines. At the end of each week, we sat together to decide which were keepers and which were not worth our time. Many were chucked in the trash can by the three of us. We all three had to agree that a piece was a keeper.

In November, Linda asked for permission to take Erik on a field trip to visit other Alaska artists. Mr. Carlson thought it was okay, so off they drove one morning. They went to see artist Jeanne Sunder, the owner of Old Post Office Art Gallery in Glennallen, along with Barb Tipton, potter, and Jane Brown, painter. When they came back at the end of the day she bolted into the classroom with Erik. The two of them looked like a couple of Cheshire cats. Their smiles went from ear to ear.

"Good timing, you two," I joked. "Have a good time playing hooky? Your field trip lasted exactly as long as the school day. How were your artist visits?"

"They loved his art!" Linda replied.

"But it's so rough and unpolished. I wouldn't pay a nickel for it. There is something missing, but I don't know what." I said.

"They sent me back with a message. They told me to make you sit down first."

"Don't be silly. Just tell me."

"Sit," she said. She walked over and gently pushed me down into a student's chair. "Okay." They said, 'Tell Mom she isn't going to have to work too much longer. Erik is going to take care of her.'"

"What?" I said, shocked. I laughed heartily.

"Yes, that's what they said," said Linda. "There is something there! I told you. His art moves me. I've known it since the first week. Now it's two months later and they agree with me."

"I have to admit, I love his Camel and the Big Eagle, but take care of me? Sure is a wonderful thought though. I'd like someone to take care of me, but I'd settle for a date," I said. I scrunched up my face with a look no man would ever want to date. "Now, that's something I haven't had in years."

Ignoring my stupid comment, she said, "They agree with us that we need better paper, more pens, and to look into copyright laws. Here's some paperwork on it." She handed me the information and started to walk away, then turned back. "Oh yeah, they think we should not just look at cards. We should look into prints, too."

I laughed over the very thought; *Erik take care of me*. Chris—absolutely he could. But Erik? He had been drawing only for a couple of months by this time. The idea was outrageous, ludicrous, and impossible. He was retarded. He was innocent. He could hardly talk. It was all a fabulous dream, but I loved the adventure of discovering my son's talents. I was having the best time of my life. This was fun!

During December the Kenny Lake Library had its Holiday Book Fair. I was gone, so Linda set up a display of Erik's artwork collection to date. We were testing the waters on marketability, and even though our process was still pretty rough, we got the response we needed. The public folks appreciated his art enough to want to buy it.

By this time I was definitely on the bandwagon to promote this young man. It was going to happen. I knew it. Doors were opening. All we had to do was to continue to listen to all the good advice that came our way when we asked our never-ending questions. We were like little children constantly asking "why?" or "how?"

Jeannie Sunder, artist and gallery owner in Glennallen, encouraged us to publish as soon as possible. She wanted his cards for the Christmas rush. We weren't ready. We still didn't know what we were doing or how to do it correctly. We talked about printing at Kinkos in

Fairbanks or Anchorage, but it was too expensive. Publishing would take thousands of dollars and should be done professionally. If it couldn't be done perfectly, I didn't want to do it at all. I sent off the first eight drawings in December to Spectrographics in California. A childhood friend owned the business. The art was eight animals, just floating in the space on a white page.

Christmas vacation finally came. We cut a little spindly spruce tree on the property and brought it into the trailer to decorate. When we had moved to Kenny Lake, I hadn't brought our ornaments. There was no place to store them. Now it was so frigid that we didn't drive to Palmer except when absolutely necessary. My dear sister in California went shopping for us and sent a box full of Christmas ornaments. We decorated the scrawny tree and hung boxes of tinsel to hide all the bare spots. It was great. We were all happy. I felt at home now. I had settled into the routine of hauling wood and water by that time. I had my boys, and in January I'd be vested in the Alaska State Teachers retirement program. I had everything I wanted except my Palmer house. My job was going great, and I loved all the variety and hard work. The fun I was having with Erik was a bonus I had never dreamed possible. You couldn't imagine a happier teacher in all of Alaska.

I spent my vacation doing schoolwork, sewing, catching up on reading, and visiting at Gay and Dave's. This couple made me feel more at home than anyone else in Kenny Lake. They were incredibly kind to us all.

We stayed home until noon of Christmas Day, then packed up the car and drove to Anchorage International Airport. I put the boys on the plane to Juneau, with a big sigh of relief. I could be irresponsible for an entire week. It was such a glorious feeling.

During vacation, I kept trying to find what I needed to do with Erik and his art. It was lacking something, but I didn't know what. Steve was scheduled to meet with Juan Munoz, Rie's son, and ask him some art business and publishing questions that I had given him. I went to an artist friend of mine, Alice Thaggard. I laid out the rough pictures on the carpeted floor of her house and she studied them. Her comments were like music to my ears. "These are really great, Linda. The only thing is he needs to ground them."

"What do you mean?" I asked.

"See how each picture is just an animal in floating in the white space? The animals have no home, no background, and no reference points. Erik needs to take each one of these and color the entire page. Fill it in. Finish them."

I looked at them with a more educated eye for the first time. "Oh, I see what you mean."

That's what they needed. I wasn't an art teacher and neither was Linda. We hadn't known that was missing. Finally, we had been led to what was needed to have a marketable product. I thought he could work on the backgrounds after Christmas, and we'd finally be ready to publish. I could hardly wait for him to come home. I was wrong, but indeed, we were one more step closer to that goal.

When Erik came back from Juneau, we made another pen run to Blaine's Art Supply to pick new colors. He'd sold enough ice cream to have about 25 colors. We were starting to buy refill ink containers to keep him going. It was averaging about $13 per color but with the pens being refillable, it was a very good long-term investment.

When school started in January of 1998, I told Linda the plan on the backgrounds. She immediately started to encourage Erik to color them. He picked up his pen and started drawing lines all around a moose. It was like asymmetrical spider webbing. Then, he started filling in the web. Suddenly, the moose drawing became something beautiful! Alice was right! Now Erik had a piece of art that I would be tempted to purchase.

I called Spectrographics and told my friend Jack to do nothing more. Everything had changed. The cards were halted for the moment. We'd missed the Christmas season, anyway. The next big sales period would be tourist season in June, so we had plenty of time to do everything right. We would have to pay for the professional scanning and printing that he had done, but that bill wouldn't come due until we were done with everything later in the year.

Though the art was more presentable, we still simply didn't know what we were doing. We were asking questions on every front. By January we still didn't have a marketable product. We needed higher quality paper, good stuff that would also work in a computer printer. Linda did the research. She called people in the valley and around the state who knew anything about quality papers. After several weeks of research on the phone between three and five every afternoon, before she had to bolt home to cook dinner, she found Nekoosa Linen, a beautiful paper. A ream was ordered immediately.

When it came, we treated that paper as if it were worth a million dollars. Each piece was precious. We went through all original black-lines that we considered keepers and printed off three of each. That would give Erik three chances for colors. If the ink blotted on the page because I refilled the pen too full, then he had another chance. Erik couldn't handle it when his black-lines were ruined. He would really get angry, and frustrated, cry, and start throwing things around. It was the one time that we saw he had a temper. It was nothing compared to many students I have worked with, but was such a surprise to see.

During the months of working long hours each day, I felt I was proving to the district that I was worth keeping around. The first day that someone hinted that my job was probably going to be short-term, I was amazed.

Mrs. Moore, the sixth grade teacher, was the first to warn me about the school district. "Linda, don't buy any property here. This district is well known for not letting new teachers get tenured."

"Why would they do that? Finding special education teachers today is not easy. No one wants to do all the extra paperwork."

"I'm just warning you to not get too attached. If they want to keep you they will move you out of Kenny Lake and up to Glennallen."

"Linda, is this true?"

"Yes, but you are great. They won't do it to you," she replied.

I wondered why a district would let me go. I worked harder than anyone and was always one of the last teachers to leave everyday. If they did decide to RIF me, at least I had my one year in. I had learned a lesson in my Kenny Lake experience. If God had put me there, he would move me where ever he wanted me to be. If I needed to move, he would arrange it. I certainly did not want to move again.

Erik was starting to enjoy the response artists and other people were giving his work. He took pleasure in all the attention. He had been used to his brother getting it all. Suddenly, everyone was talking about Erik. Things were changing. He took it very calmly. He would just smile and look down modestly as discussions went on around him.

We had to understand copyright law, especially for the cards. Erik and I were led to visit Christopher and Wick Wright in Glennallen. After introducing myself to the tall, thin lady, I said, "Linda told me that you would help me figure out how to copyright Erik's art."

Wick pulled out forms from a large filing cabinet that read; Form VA. For a Work of the Visual Arts, United States Copyright Office. The form looked overwhelming. I wasn't sure how to fill it out.

She said, "It's not that hard; you can do it. The main thing is to remember to send two photos of every art piece that you want to copyright. You can secure the rights on twenty art pieces for only $20. It is a great investment."

"Should I copyright everything Erik does?" I asked.

"No, just the things that you sell or publish. If it is in your hands, there is no need to. Everything else you copyright. This will protect Erik's art from people who like to take advantage of artists."

"This could really add up over time. We will need a safe place to keep all this legal paperwork, in case of fire."

"That would be wise. For now you could start with a poor man's copyright and then do the more expensive Federal copyright later. You photograph the art in question, seal it in envelopes, and then mail it to yourself. The post office date on the envelope will work in court, if necessary, as long as you never open the envelope." (We kept the early copyright paperwork double wrapped in plastic Ziploc bags in the middle of our sixteen cubic foot freezer for years until we purchased a fireproof safe.) I surely was grateful for the free guidance and advice they gave us.

Many people in the Copper River Valley gave us ideas of where to look for funding. Some thought the Down's Syndrome Congress might want to use Erik and his art in a fund-raising effort. He would gain visibility and recognition. They told us about foundation charitable trusts, which might be another source of funding. There were so many avenues. Linda took some; I took others. One person couldn't do it all and teach school. This project was branching off like a Sitka spruce. We had to hold on to the strong base and pick which branch would be best to follow. We had so much information that we never followed up some leads, like the Copper Valley Economic Development Council which might have wanted to be involved in the development of the art business or might have become a grant source. Names were filed and sometimes forgotten. Because of the confusion, we were always saying to each other, "Now, who is this person?" or "What did you find out from so and so?" Teaching is hard enough to keep straight but you add on a project like this one and your memory can lapse.

During that winter and spring Linda was going one way and I was going another, all for Erik. We would have meetings after school to share the information we'd gathered and redirect our efforts in whichever way needed. We started prioritizing everything. We had lists everywhere and often lost them. After one of our "Now who is this or that?" meetings, we decided we needed To Do Lists, that we couldn't lose. Linda and I took two long pieces of butcher paper and hung them on the front of the closet behind Erik's desk. Linda wrote our things to do with a broad felt tip marker so we could easily read the reminders from across the room. As we accomplished our goals, we happily checked them off.

I would frequently say, "I'm going to the computer lab to work on the black-lines that Erik drew this week. First though, I need to finish doing my data for the day. I'll see you tomorrow." We would each dash off to our various work sites for Erik, and also, somehow, get our work done for all the other important students.

Linda would scurry home as usual about 4:55 to take care of her husband, and Erik and I would continue in the peace and quiet of an empty classroom, listening to the rattling, banging, and popping of the ancient oil-fired furnace as it worked valiantly to keep the old building above freezing. We could stay only as long as our bladders would allow some days, since the plumbing was periodically frozen. We either had to put on all our winter gear and walk over to the high school to use the bathroom, or go home for the night. I was starting to get a real handle on the job and was now generally finished by 6:30.

One thing needed was a portfolio. We started two of them. One was just of Erik's drawings. The pictures that were glued on black paper for the school board meeting in November had been put in plastic page protectors and collected into a big three-ring binder. Samples of everything were saved.

Names, dates, business cards and information gathered were also put in another art portfolio. We didn't have time to write things nicely or bother to spell correctly. Notes were just thrown in the plastic sheet protectors in the correct month to possibly be organized in the future. We didn't want to lose any leads that might help Erik. People were telling us to set vocational goals, objectives, figure costs, time frames, and find vendors. We needed help. By March we had taken it as far as we could. We had outgrown the original idea of just selling cards. I asked people where to turn next.

Chapter Eleven
Reaching Beyond

We pursued Vocational Rehabilitation by calling and sending letters and art samples. Mrs. Fox came to visit us from the Wasilla office. She liked what she saw and said she would help us get our business going. Nothing happened, though, because during the next few months, Vocational Rehabilitation was reorganized. Nevertheless, we continued to pursue their help. When I slowed down, Linda would pick it up and run with it, and vice versa. What a team! Months later Erik was assigned David Kavasagar from the Voc. Rehab. Anchorage office as his case manager.

Linda and I sent samples of Erik's art to the Alaska State Council on the Arts. We were so disappointed. The people acted like Erik didn't belong with normal artists. They called him an "Outsider artist," an artist who is not trained by a university or art school. If Erik were too disabled to be a part of the "normal" art world, then I feared he might never make it to the professional level. To be an artist in a regular gallery, did he have to be trained?

All of the samples that we sent were passed on to Dr. W. of Very Special Arts Alaska, an affiliate of an organization that promoted arts around the world for people with disabilities. Erik certainly qualified under their requirements. From those early samples, there was no way that Dr. W could even have a feel for all that Erik could do, and yet one day he said on the phone to Linda, "I will take Erik Behnke to Washington D.C, and the Kennedy Center." She ran back to our classroom to tell us. "Can you believe it? He wants to send Erik's art to D.C.!" screamed Linda.

We danced around the room and both hugged Erik and he giggled between us in the excitement. After calming down, we had so many questions! We wanted to trust Dr. W. but truth be told we knew no more about the man than we did Erik's skill. Dr. W. had to be legitimate if he was a director of Very Special Arts, Alaska, didn't he? Should we trust him to help Erik? Maybe Erik was too disabled to compete in the regular art world. Eventually Linda and I talked ourselves into thinking that Dr. W. was the lead we needed in the big search for Erik's success. We were traveling on a gigantic dream machine. We laughed excitedly every time we talked art, and Erik loved it.

By March local people were starting to want to buy Erik's pieces, but we weren't ready. We didn't know if we should sell his art, how to sell it, or what to do with his Special Needs Trust or Social Security if we did. We had more questions than we had answers, and in the end, decided to do nothing. It was better to just hold on to everything than to sell too early, or the wrong way, and regret it later.

Kenny Lake needed a Special Olympics team, so I started one. I had been an area director, head coach or coach for Special Olympics Alaska for 10 years. After months of practice, Team Kenny Lake was off to the State Winter Games in Anchorage. When cheering Erik at the start line for the 3K cross country ski race on Saturday, I ran into Terry, an old friend from Ketchikan.

"Linda, I heard Erik is doing art now," he said. "I'm on the board for the 2001 Special Olympic World Winter Games. You ought to submit a proposal with Erik's art."

"For a logo?"

"They already accepted a logo from a team of graphic artists." He showed me the images. They were computer-generated and nothing like Erik's work.

"Erik could do better than that. I'll encourage him to work on it. We're always looking for new ideas."

"Maybe a poster for each event."

"What are the events?" I asked.

"The usual winter games plus snowshoeing," he said. "Erik might not know what that event looks like. They only use short snowshoes."

"So nothing like the giant rawhide ones used in the Bush?"

"Look on the Internet if you want more information. Got to go." He skied off toward his team. My mind was going crazy with new ideas for Erik to explore. It was time to branch out from Alaskan animals anyway. Athletes in motion might be fun for him.

Back at school my class was running like clockwork by spring. In the first hour, I had two students doing algebra, four junior high students doing written reading assignments, and three little second graders doing math with money. I walked around the room, working with students individually as they raised their hands for help. Rumors had spread about Erik's art, and people wanted to watch him work when they had the chance.

The second graders were all watching and waving their arms to get my attention.

"Yes?" I asked one little eight-year-old boy.

"We're finished with our math assignment. Can we watch Erik?"

I nodded my head, yes and the three quietly walked over to sit next to Erik. He said nothing, but did occasionally look up at them. He was shy, but okay with them.

More and more students were interested. Another day a sixth-grade girl stuck her head into the door of our room. "School's out. Can we watch you work, Erik?"

Erik nodded calmly. This had become a normal part of his life. He continued to work quietly. Four children sat next to him and watched silently.

Another day in April, a woman with two little children came to our room to watch. "Erik, I love your art. It is so colorful. Can I buy it?"

Erik didn't answer her. When he was working, nothing distracted him. He was on the job and he was a man hard at work.

"I still have to figure out how to run his business," I said. "It's complicated. Maybe, after I meet with my lawyer."

"I just love it."

"Sorry. I'll make sure you know when the time comes." I loved it that people were open and receptive to him.

In late April, two Kenny Lake men in Carhartts came in and indicated with sign language that they would like to watch Erik work. They stood beside him and watched over his shoulder. One man was clean cut with short hair. The other had long gray hair that stuck out despite his homemade knit watch cap. His Carhartts were dirty. Both smiled as they watched. Erik looked up at the men and then went on quietly smiling to himself. He was okay with them, not shy at all now. He was growing more confident and proud of his work everyday.

The rumor was out in Copper River Valley that something very special was happening in little Kenny Lake School. People were calling and asking Linda questions on Erik's art progress. Linda knew all the locals and was a natural for handling the local public relations. I had lived all around Alaska and knew people everywhere else so I decided to focus on the rest of the state.

Erik standing near our trailer. This field had horses in it all winter. Kenny Lake is a farming area and this was a hayfield which was bailed in August.

Erik always had to have an area on the floor at home where he could spread his books out and play with writing and coloring using his markers. Even after a long day at school, he would bring his pens home and work on his art until bedtime.

Chris and Erik stop for a picture break and walk during the long drives between Kenny Lake and Anchorage.

Chris in the Anchorage Airport before he left to go live with his dad in Juneau.

Mrs. Tansy made a birthday cake for every student in Kenny Lake Jr. High and High school. This is Chris on his birthday with Newly and Rhu, two of his friends. Rhu said, "Mrs. Tansy has made enough cakes to feed a small country."

Erik doing his art in our classroom. Linda gave Erik her desk to work on so he would be by the window and could enjoy the wildlife while he worked.

Our Kenny Lake team hug. Even today, these boys are kind and loving to each other like this when they meet at State Special Olympic events in Anchorage. (above)

Team Kenny Lake Special Olympics, They were a very loving group. From Right to left, Levi Wenger, Marlene Wenger, Chris Olsen, Erik Behnke, and the author, Linda Thompson. (above)

Erik receiving his gold medal in cross country skiing at the 2000 Alaska Special Olympic State Winter Games. (left)

Chapter Twelve
Going to Galleries

Spring break came. While all the other teachers went on vacation, I was still working. Working, by this time, was something like living a daydream full time. It was time to test the art in a bigger pond. Juan Munoz had told us that Erik needed 45 to 50 originals in his portfolio before he tried to sell to the galleries. He now had 46.

Erik and I drove to Anchorage to visit art galleries and see what the owners had to say. The artists in Copper River told us to go to Artique, a well-known reputable art gallery that might be interested in Erik's art. As we were headed up the street, we found ourselves outside Stephan's Fine Art. I knew nothing about art galleries. I knew only about Eskimo and Indian art, but nothing about what was in Anchorage.

We walked into Stephan's and looked around for a minute. It's like I was blind; I didn't know what I was looking at, much less the subject matter or value of anything. Quickly, a young lady approached. Our casual dress from Kenny Lake probably told her we didn't have thousands of dollars to spend.

"May I help you?" she asked.

"Yes, is the gallery owner here?" I asked her.

"No, he is out of the state, buying in Seattle," the young lady answered. "Is there something I can do for you?"

"I wanted to speak to the owner about Erik. He is an artist." I gestured to my son who was already tired of walking, happy to sit and rock for a while on the carpeted floor. I grabbed him under the arm tightly and made him stand politely in the gallery. "Erik is from the Copper River area. This is our first time to Anchorage and I am interested in finding a market for his work for next summer."

"I have worked here quite a while. Do you have his portfolio? I'll probably be able to tell you if the owners will be interested in his type of art."

I reached into the computer case that I was using as a briefcase, pulled out a manila file folder from school, and handed the originals to her. She handled the originals very carefully. After looking at three or four drawings, she called to another young man that worked there. "Hey, come look at these!"

The young man came over and the two gawked.

"Did you really draw these, Erik?" she asked.

Erik smiled and nodded.

"These are really great, Erik."

I told them he was a new artist from the small community of Kenny Lake.

"These are really wonderful. I doubt that Stephan's will be interested in this form of art though. Look around you. This place sells very expensive oil paintings, and some sculpture."

Suddenly, I was like Eve after she ate the apple; my eyes were opened to the type of gallery into which we had walked. I realized that everything I could see was over $1,000. There was nothing like Erik's drawings to be seen. We were out of our league.

"This is the wrong gallery for Erik's art, but it is wonderful. There are other galleries in Anchorage that would probably be very interested in his art. Don't give up here," said the young man.

"Oh yes," said the young lady.

As I took the folder back I asked, "Could you advise us where we should try next?"

They looked at each other as they thought. The young man said, "Why don't you try Decker Art? It is right across the street. Might be a good one," he said.

I looked out the windows and saw the Decker sign. "Thanks for your words of encouragement. Erik, let's go there next." We walked out into the cool spring air. I stopped to zip up our jackets tightly around our necks. Spring is a time for colds because it is so much warmer than winter and many Alaskans think it's really summer. Our bodies are used to being at eighty degrees inside our parkas, and the sudden change to the thirty-five to forty degree outside temperature is too much of a change. I didn't have time to bother with spring colds for either of us.

Decker Art was a let-down after being in Stephan's. Decker Art was in the middle of remodeling or something. I have never been there since to know what they look like in the summer, but that spring day, they were a mess. Wall displays were not up. Wadded-up paper littered the floor as if they were moving. Very little was up for a customer to view, much less purchase. I could tell by the location that they were probably a viable business; we had just walked in at the wrong time.

After the "innocent Eve" experience at Stephan's, I really wanted to get a feel for the type of gallery Decker Art was. Would Erik's art fit? Because of the level of disarray, I honestly could not tell. I approached a man in his late twenties and asked, "Is there any chance I could speak to the owner?"

"The owners are down in Portland at a show," he said. "Can I help you?"

"This is Erik Behnke. He is a young artist from Kenny Lake. We are wondering what galleries think of his art. We would like to find a market for next summer."

Erik was really tired of walking. Everytime I let go of his hand, he quickly sat down on the floor of the gallery and rocked back and forth. This was not the time for him to go into La-La Land. I firmly grabbed him up off the floor and secured my arm in his in a way that I had mastered over the years that fused the two of us into one body. There was no way he could wiggle out of my vise-grip arm hold to slide back down to the floor and space out. He giggled at the attention and stood there, testing his strength against mine every few minutes.

"I'd be glad to take a look and give you an opinion, for what it's worth. I can usually spot something the owners would like. Do you have his portfolio?"

He carefully looked at the pictures. "Erik, these are very nice. Have you ever thought about children's books? His art is so colorful and striking. It would be wonderful for illustrations," he said as he looked at the forty-six different pictures.

"I don't know if he could do book illustrations. It would be very difficult for him to do what someone else told him to do. It is a thought, though. I think he could illustrate a book, but only if the book was written after the art was drawn." I explained how he worked on each piece, did what he wanted, when and how he wanted or we ended up with him in tears. A book seemed like months of agony for both of us at that point.

"The owners might be very interested in Erik's art. They'll be back next week. Could you leave his portfolio for them to look at?"

Absolutely not, was my immediate thought. Erik had spent the school year working on those originals, and there was no way I was going to leave them with this stranger. Besides, we still had hours before the other galleries in Anchorage were going to close. Even if I didn't have another day off for two months, I wouldn't leave it.

"Could you please give me a business card? I could contact them when I return in a month or so," I said. He wrote notes to his bosses about Erik.

"Sure. I am really serious. Erik's art would be great for children's books. Don't forget that," he reminded me.

"Thanks for taking the time to help," I said. "Say 'bye,' Erik,"

"Bye," said Erik. We put the portfolio back in my computer case and walked out.

"Well, even if we don't find the right gallery today, at least we are making the effort, Erik."

Erik smiled at me and snuggled closer as we walked down the street, the chilly spring winds blowing our hair all around.

We stopped at the corner of Sixth and G and looked down the street. There on the corner of Fifth was another art gallery I had never been in. "Aurora Fine Art. That place looks interesting, Erik. Let's see what it looks like inside."

We walked quickly, anxiously looking forward to getting out of the crisp air and into a warm place. Erik and I walked into a gallery full of the most beautiful two- and three-dimensional art. They had glass, ceramic, ivory, bone, framed prints and originals, cards, everything. It had a collection of the finest, no phony Alaskan art mass-produced in China. I would have loved to have every piece in my beautiful home in Palmer. It was all too good for the house trailer in Kenny Lake.

As I looked around, holding tightly to Erik, I spotted a beautiful woman with dark brown shoulder-length hair behind the counter. She had glasses on and was concentrating on paperwork in front of her. By this time, I knew this was the kind of gallery in which I really wanted Erik's art. Erik just wanted to sit down. I walked up to her and asked if I could speak to the owner of the gallery.

"I am the owner. My name is Diane Louise."

"This is Erik Behnke. He's my student at Kenny Lake School. I would just like to know what you think of his art and if you would be interested in selling it."

She opened up the manila folder full of originals and started to look at a few of the pieces and stopped. "Who are you to Erik? Just his teacher?"

"I'm also his mom and his legal guardian." Erik found a chair next to the glass counter filled with hundreds of very expensive ivory carvings. He sat and watched me watch the lady.

"Oh, good." She continued to look with her head tilted down and eyes focusing intently on the pieces in the folder. She studied each piece slowly before turning to the next.

I wasn't sure what she was thinking. I knew I loved everything in that folder. No matter what she thought, I was now a total believer in this twenty-year-old man.

Suddenly she stopped, looked up at us both, and asked in her soft, kind, voice, "Erik, did you really draw these wonderful pieces of art?"

We both looked at Erik, for once happily sitting still.

He studied us as though he was translating the question into a language he could understand. Finally he said clearly, "Yes." Then he started to rock gently in his chair. He was very focused on what was happening here. He wasn't off in another land mentally. He seemed to recognize that this was important.

"Erik, you do very nice work. How do you do it?"

He didn't respond so I said, "He uses Tria Pantone Markers. It is the only art medium that he is interested in using."

"Has he been doing this long?"

"We just discovered that he had this gift six months ago. He works everyday from three to ten hours on his art and loves doing it."

She asked many more questions about how he did it, and I filled her in on his program at Kenny Lake School as she slowly went through the portfolio. Suddenly she stopped turning the pictures. Her eyes focused off the page for a few seconds and then drifted back. She hadn't even finished looking at all forty-six of them. She very calmly put her hands together and looked at us as though to say something very important.

"Erik, I really like your work. I would like to make an announcement. I would like to be the first gallery to introduce Erik Behnke to the world."

It was like I was hit with a bullet. Shock! I started weeping with joy in the middle of that beautiful gallery. She liked his art! She was a very successful gallery owner and obviously knew about art. I was glad the place was empty at the moment, as I made a total fool of myself.

Tears poured down my face, and my nose ran like I had the worst cold in the world. Of course, Erik started to cry, too. He always cried when I cried. For his entire life I had always had to hide my emotions from him. That day I just let them flow, even as I tried to thank her.

"Y- Y-You have no idea what your words mean to me. P- P- People have never thought Erik could amount to anything. This is a dream come true." *The World! The World! She wants to introduce him to the world. Wow!* I kept thinking.

Diane came out from behind the glass counter and gave us both a big hug. I was dizzy. Erik was worried. He didn't understand what she had said, but he did understand that Mom was upset and he'd only seen me happy for the whole school year.

"It's okay, Erik. Diane really likes your art. She thinks it's great and wants everyone to think so too. I am just very happy for you." I used a couple of Kleenex on his nose. He might be an artist with pens, but he couldn't clean his runny nose without smearing it all the way to his ear.

After all tears were dried up and Erik and I calmed down, Diane went behind the counter again and got a calendar out. "Okay, we need to have an art show this summer. How about June?" she said.

"Old Post Office Gallery in Glennallen has talked about a show for Erik in June but the owner, Jeanne Sunder, has never picked a date. Maybe we should schedule another time. She has been really great about helping guide Erik," I said. "Besides, I don't know if the cards will be back from the printer by then. All kinds of delays so far."

"Do you want to sell originals?" she asked.

"I don't know. I guess so," I said.

This was the beginning of a new stage of learning about art. Up to this time, I had been learning what Erik could and should do to have a marketable product. I'd started to learn about publishing by trying to print the cards. Cards weren't intimidating in the least. On the other hand, I knew nothing about selling originals or prints. There were few books on the subject of marketing art. I was going to have to learn by asking people I trusted. Whom could I trust? Dr. W., from Very Special Arts, was the only one I knew at that time. Diane seemed honest to me. I had a feeling that God had led me to find her first. I was certain it would be okay.

Diane, Erik, and I became very good friends and business associates that day. She quickly realized our limitations. Since I knew nothing, I dragged my feet and rushed into nothing. If this was to be a career for Erik, he had a lifetime to develop it. There was no need to rush. Dr. W. eventually came out to visit us in Kenny Lake that May and helped us decide to not sell originals, not just yet. Printing cost an arm and a leg. I could easily spend $6,000 on a few prints. The cards were already costing more than $3000. My personal expenses were mounting. I expected I was going to have to purchase a place to live for the next winter. I couldn't spend $10,000 on Erik's art business.

Right after spring break, Linda and I experimented with Erik taking orders for hand-done originals. He would only get $25 for each original. Erik's speech teacher, Deb Fortune from Big Delta, had been watching his progress all year. She really wanted to be the first buyer and had money ready to spend. We were tempted but Linda and I learned Erik's limits. Deb ordered certain colors.

"Come on, Erik. Deb wants these shades of green, blue, and pink. You can do it like she wants," said Linda. "Here they are."

Erik looked at her and tried to pick up another color.

"No, Erik, she wants these colors." She put the pens in his hand. He dropped them and once again tried to pick up the color he wanted. Several more times she tried to encourage him to use the ordered colors and finally he started to cry. She also felt like crying. She was doing what she thought we needed to do for the buyer but it obviously wasn't going to work. Erik's put his head was down on the table. Linda felt very guilty for pushing him and eventually gave up the fight. It wasn't worth it. Both were exhausted with the ordeal.

After school, we had our usual discussions about the day's progress and problems.

"If Erik doesn't like doing his art, then he might as well be folding towels in a Laundromat," I said. "You can lead a horse to water but you can't make it drink. The same thing goes for Erik."

We were doing this so he could have a profession he'd love to do. How many people get to do what they love? This was our only goal—for him to be happy in a viable profession that he loved. It had taken me many years and many different career starts to find something I loved to do. If we could luck out with Erik and find something enjoyable from the beginning, what a blessing that would be.

Erik had to be trusted. Just because he was severely retarded didn't mean he didn't know what he needed to do when it came to his art. From this moment on, we never suggested colors. If people wanted an order with specific standards, we would reply, "Sorry, we will encourage Erik to try on this project, but if he isn't interested in it, it won't happen." It was too bad, but making money was not the object here. Buyers would have to take whatever Erik was in the mood to give. Erik was a free spirit, and absolutely no one should or could dictate directions to him. Erik created on personal motivation. We were only there to aid him if he needed or wanted assistance. Erik was the artist-in-charge.

Somehow, though our professions were different, we were very much alike. I often felt the same way when school principals tried to order me around at work. I learned to just do what I had to do to please them. I never changed my way of thinking. Fortunately Erik never felt the social pressure I have felt, since he is a totally free entrepreneur.

The next day we told Deb Fortune that the experiment had failed. She would have to wait for a print. At that time, there was nothing for sale, and we didn't have the funding to print anything. She was disappointed, but accepted our decision. She really loved Erik and his art.

Chapter Thirteen
Working Toward Marketing

In late March, my principal called me into his office. Until that day, I completely trusted Copper River School District and had no fear of the administration. I'd worked for many school districts off and on during a period of 27 years. I had seen administrations do some pretty odd things, but up until that March I had only observed a top-quality administration in Copper River Schools. I had heard many rumors from teachers and parents about "problems," but had learned never to pay attention to gossip. I had no idea why he wanted to talk to me.

He closed the door as I sat down. Then he went behind his cluttered desk. He said, "Linda, I have been told to inform you that your job will be ending at the end of the school year in May."

I sat there, shocked. No district had ever done that to me. I took a deep breath and said, "What! Why?"

"You are not tenured, and another teacher from Glennallen has been on a year's sabbatical leave. When a teacher takes a year off, they are promised a job when they return. You were the last one hired last fall, so your job is the one the District is going to offer her.

I want you to know that I feel you have done a wonderful job here at Kenny Lake, and we will miss you. I tried to help you keep your job, but I had no choice. I would recommend that you go to the Alaska Teachers Job Fair in April and find another position."

I was totally in shock. Here I had a great job that I could focus on, in a good school where my boys were getting a good education in a safe environment. I was happier than I had been in years and now this. Was I supposed to go back to being a miserable substitute teacher in Palmer? Before Kenny Lake, substitute teaching was marginally acceptable. No! I didn't want to return to working for pennies, barely able to pay my bills. I also didn't belong back in the Bush. My boys needed more than that. Why was this happening? What did God have planned for me, I wondered?

I left the office, not in tears, more in dismay. I couldn't believe it. Why should I try so hard when the district superintendent and board didn't really care? Many teachers, staff, and community members had warned me to never expect to stay long. New teachers were always temporary at Kenny Lake. They said that if I made it to tenure, they would be surprised. They always discouraged me from buying property, thinking I would certainly be let go. They were right.

I truly felt that God had had a hand in getting me there, and it wasn't time for me to leave. I couldn't trust any other teacher to work as hard as I did with Erik and this was the best situation that I had found to help Chris with his 504 plan. It was set up to encourage him to always wear his Comtex unit (an electronic system for both him and his teachers) so he could hear his teachers better. No other special education or regular education teachers cared about it like I did. They allowed him to forget it and to fail. A mom doesn't do that.

I was just a little pawn in a political game. From what I could gather from long-time teachers, even though I loved my job, it was considered a tough duty position. Rumor was, the teacher in Glennallen had been assigned to my position as a form of punishment for something she had said before she went on sabbatical leave. Assigning her to my job when she lived fifty miles away was a form of discipline, or payback. Driving that far in the severe cold (50 to 60 below 0 F) was extremely dangerous. Teachers who were vocal against an administration, were sometimes disciplined this way, but I was the one losing my job and I had done nothing wrong.

I really wanted to stay in Kenny Lake, not only because of my own family, but also because of another family that had lost all trust in the public schools. They had two sons with intensive needs. We had become good friends and I really didn't want someone ruining all the progress I had made with helping the youngest boy get in school for the first time. He was nine years old, and he needed to start as soon as possible. I felt committed to this child.

No matter how I looked at this, I was still hurt.

In April, I took off a couple of days and went to the Job Fair in Anchorage. I have always disliked the meat market atmosphere of the fair. I had found that if you didn't look or act a certain way, you would never get a job. Dressy clothes, fancy hairdos, and makeup always had been low on my priority list, but I decided to give it my best shot. Unfortunately, even when I try sometimes, I still shoot myself in the foot.

I rented a room in the Captain Cook Hotel, where the job fair was held. That way, I could make sure I looked great. The morning the fair opened I got up early, curled my hair, ironed my grey pinstriped suit, and carefully put on makeup. I was going to look fabulous.

When it was time for the fair to start, I calmly walked out the door with my black three-inch heels, business suit, bright red silk blouse and briefcase. I pushed the button on the elevator and when the door opened, there stood four administrators I knew from Palmer. I decided to be aloof and ignore them. They were the last district I would ever want to work for. I stepped in and stood right in front of them with my back to them.

Eventually, the elevator made it down to level one. I quickly walked out and started down the marble-floored hallway. People were looking at me strangely, but I decided it was just because I looked so good.

A woman of about thirty, walked right up and stopped me. "Do you realize that you still have a few pink curlers in your hair?"

I freaked out and immediately went to a wall beside a very large plant and started yanking them out of my hair as fast as possible. I had left in five, more than enough to make a fool of myself. The woman tried to calm me down.

"It's okay. It's okay. You haven't talked to any districts yet, have you?"

"No, I just came down."

"Good. Shake your head. Your hair looks wild and natural. It's okay, relax."

"Thank you for telling me. I'm just not used to paying any attention to my looks. It's not important to me most of the time."

Once she was sure I wasn't going to die from embarrassment, she walked on. I stuffed the pink sponge curlers in my briefcase and immediately went in the lady's room to confirm her opinion. Fashion humiliation always seemed to be part of my life.

I interviewed with several districts, but if Erik was an artist, Homer, a noted artist community at the tip of the Kenai Peninsula, might be where I should go. Another advantage to Homer was its warmer climate moderated by the warm North Pacific Ocean.

I met a fantastic couple of men from Kenai Peninsula School District, Rick McCrum and Roy Anderson, and interviewed with them. Before the end of the second day, they offered me a contract to teach elementary special education in the very town I wanted, Homer. It meant a huge cut in pay, but I was still excited. The contract had to be approved by the school board and superintendent, so I didn't have to sign anything immediately. That was fine with me. Though the doors seemed to be closing in my beloved Kenny Lake, maybe Homer was where we were really supposed to be in the future. I wasn't about to second-guess ever again what God wanted from me. He knew what I needed.

I went back to the little trailer, to Kenny Lake, feeling good about the offer, but dreading the prospect of making the 500-mile move. I had just gotten settled in Kenny Lake. Packing up and driving back to Palmer and then another 280 miles south to Homer was more than I wanted to endure.

Development of the art business continued. I kept thinking about what we should do next. I was content with the idea of selling just cards. This was all I could imagine. Prints would cost thousands. They were worth only twenty-five dollars apiece at that time. Over and over, Linda and I discussed whether we should sell originals in Anchorage. Finally, I made the decision to sell them. I drove into Anchorage and went to Aurora Fine Art to see Diane.

"Diane, I would like to sell Erik's originals. Would you like to buy them?" I asked.

She looked at me like a businesswoman and said she would. I handed her the folder, and she proceeded to go through it carefully, picking out the best. All ones that I didn't want to give away. It was like my heart was being torn out of my body. Twenty-five dollars was a giveaway, but I didn't know that. It seemed like a good deal for Erik. If he were going to sell his art, then this seemed like the next step. (I didn't find any books on being an art representative in 1998. I learned by the school of hard knocks. This was part of my education.)

I stood there, feeling that I was right on selling them, but like every mother who discovers something absolutely wonderful about their child, I didn't want to let them go. There were about fifty originals done perfectly with the correct paper, pens, centering, etc., in the folder that day. I was sick to my stomach.

As she slowly picked out about twenty-five of them and put them in a separate pile, she suddenly stopped and stated very firmly, "No!" She put all of the originals back in the folder and quickly closed it as if it were a temptation that she had to control. She handed it back to me and said, "Don't ever tempt me like that again. I could buy these from you and make a great deal of money from them, but that's not what's important here."

My jaw dropped.

"What is important is the career of this wonderful artist. I'm going to teach you what you need to know to help Erik."

Suddenly I realized that God was right in that room. He was protecting Erik from being taken advantage of by anyone, since I didn't know what I was doing. God was his manager. Diane was being guided to do what was right for Erik, not just right for her business.

"You shouldn't release ownership of originals to anyone at this time. Maintain control for Erik's future." She explained this was Erik's nest egg and it was my job to protect it and manage it wisely. It would be wiser if I made prints of them and sold only the prints.

"But I can't afford prints right now. I lost my job, and we have to move to Homer, unless they give my job back to me in the next couple of weeks," I said.

"I have an idea that may work. When are you coming to town again?"

"Next weekend if you want me to."

"I'll do some calling around and see what I can do."

I had no idea what Diane had in mind at that time, but I'd learned a valuable lesson that day. Here was a smart businesswoman, but she loved and cared for Erik and me. She didn't want to take advantage of Erik's innocence or my ignorance. I left Anchorage totally grateful that God had led us to this wonderful woman. She would do only what was right. She was going to help me understand what I needed to know. From this point on, I never worried about being taken advantage of by Diane. She has always been wonderfully honest, and truthful, and a great friend to my family.

April continued to be an exciting time for Erik. I wanted to help him as much as possible while I was still at Kenny Lake. Sometimes though, I wondered if I would put so much effort into the art if it weren't part of my job. I often thought, the school district might as well get its money's worth out of me. Erik will only benefit from this hard-working teacher. I certainly didn't know what would happen the next year if I weren't in charge of his program any longer.

Next weekend, I once again drove the three of us to Anchorage. I left the boys at the homestead with Grandma and went to see Diane. She had approached a businessman she respected at Arctic Office Products. I went along for the ride and the education. As the beautiful woman discussed Erik's art with the man, I watched and learned about publishing, color, presentation, and the business of reproduction. I was amazed when she negotiated a deal. He paid for the first 600 prints of Erik's art as a donation to help my son, a new and upcoming artist. Now there was something with which to start the business. I couldn't stop smiling. I wanted to hug and kiss that gentleman, but refrained from being too emotional.

After the printing was complete, Diane took ten of each of the images so she could prepare for the first show. She told me to send her a bill. I agreed to do it, but told her I would wait until I had talked to my lawyer. I wanted to set the business up so it wouldn't hurt Erik.

Maybe this art business wouldn't succeed; maybe it would. As far as I was concerned, the only thing that was important was that Erik was happy and felt that he had an important place in life. Art was the perfect way to meet those desires. The business was simply a means to an end.

School continued to demand long hours of my time from Monday through Friday. I made a vow that I would have a life when I went home. I refused to take any more work to the trailer at night. All work stayed at school except the development of Erik's career. I crossed the line into overtime happily when it came to working for Erik. For something like Erik's career to develop, it took extraordinary dedication. I knew a lot of teachers who worked overtime, and very hard, but none of them would work until 9 or 10 every night for a single student.

I decided I simply couldn't lose my job. This school district couldn't just throw me away, and we needed them too much. Erik was scheduled to graduate in spring of 1999, just a year away. I thought about staying as a substitute teacher for that year, but knew I couldn't afford to do that. I wouldn't earn enough money to pay my rent and fuel oil bills. I didn't know what to do, but I had to stay.

Art-wise, things were really happening. Dr. W of Very Special Arts Alaska set up an appointment to see Erik's art. He was going to be in the region in May. On the day of his arrival, we took Erik's originals in sheet protectors and taped them all around the room on the walls. We wanted to wow him with Erik's work when he walked in the room.

The short, stocky man who walked in wearing boots, blue jeans, and a plaid wool shirt, certainly did not have the cultured art gallery look that we expected.

"Welcome," I said

"Oh, you have his work all up on the walls."

He immediately started his tour around the room while Linda, Erik and I just smiled. He studied each piece before moving on to the next. Even though nothing was matted or framed, he was instantly able to grasp Erik's style.

"These are wonderful. Is all of his work small like this?"

"Yes," I said. "He only likes to work with small paper. Maybe he will do larger pieces in the future."

"I love this Loon In A Lake," he said as he studied it. Finally he completed his tour and we all sat down around one of the classroom tables and began to ask each other questions.

"How can I help you?"

"We have a lot of questions as to the direction we need to go with all this," I said.

"Some gallery owners want to sell Erik's originals. We don't know what to do with them. Is it wise to sell them or should we hold on to them?" Linda asked.

"And if we do sell them, what are they worth?" I questioned. "Is it wise to sell originals at low prices just to get his name out there? We want to promote his career and not harm it but have no idea what is the right thing to do."

He adjusted his seat in the hard little school chairs. "If I were you, I would hold on to all originals. You don't know where this is going. Don't let go of them until you are ready," he said. "It could be years."

I was immediately relieved. This was what I really wanted to hear. It reconfirmed what Diane had said. All the people who wanted to buy could be told, "No sorry, they are not for sale at this time," since Dr. W. thought it was wise. As a mother, I didn't like the idea of letting go of any of the originals. I was so proud of each and every one of those early paintings. To me, they were priceless. Even today, almost 10 years later, we have never sold any of those originals from 1997-1999. They are locked up in a dark dry safe.

We talked for about an hour. When he left, he wanted to take ten of our six hundred prints for free, because he was going to take them to Washington D.C. during June of 1998 and try to get us a showing. We were so excited about Erik having a show in a gallery on the east coast. Might it happen? That remained to be seen.

Kenai Schools didn't send me the contract in a time frame I expected; I didn't worry about it. They wanted to hire me, and I knew my records were in excellent order. They'd send it eventually. Secretly I really didn't want to sign. Once I signed, it was a contract that couldn't be broken without the risk of permanently losing my Alaskan Teachers Certificate. Once I received a contract, I had thirty days to sign it or lose the option. The longer Kenai took, the more time Copper River Schools had to straighten out its problems with the teacher who was supposed to take my place. Each day, I checked my mailbox on the highway and happily found it empty of the signature card notifying the arrival of the delayed contract. I would have to drive all the way to Copper Center, about thirty miles, to the nearest post office to pick up the certified letter.

I didn't call to question for weeks. It was fine.

Rumors were flowing heavily from Glennallen that the teacher who was supposed to take my job was very unhappy with her contract offer. Rumor was she was going to try to get a job with another district.

At night I prayed, "Dear God, please guide Mrs.____ to the perfect job that would bless her in every way. I know she doesn't want Kenny Lake, and God, I certainly do. Please let me stay here to teach Erik, and help little L's family so he can go to school for the first time."

I was smart enough to know, from previous experience, I would be led to whatever I needed. If there was something better than Kenny Lake out there, then God would lead me that way. Nonetheless, I really wanted to just stay put and hoped that was what God had for a plan. It was too much work to think about moving. Little did I know how much work it would take just to stay.

Early in May, winter finally broke. Things started to really melt during the day. The ground was still frozen, but all the snow melted off the roof of the trailer. It was so wonderful to hear water dripping off the roof onto the ice below.

After a few days, the snow on the horse fields to the east of our trailer started to thaw and the water started to flow down the hill. I had never noticed the terrain around the trailer until we came home from work one Wednesday and found that the trailer was suddenly in the middle of a runoff stream. I didn't have my breakup boots on, and the water was so deep that I couldn't get to the trailer. The trail to the door was a bubbling brook.

We took firewood and dropped chunks in front of us as we walked, building a temporary trail to walk on. That night we opened all the windows and listened to robins singing all night, and water gurgling and bubbling around the house on its way down the gentle slope. It was such a glorious feeling to be part of nature for a change. It was warm enough to enjoy the outdoors again. How wonderful spring is each year after the dark and the cold winter. "Glorious" is the only word to describe it.

In the middle of May, things changed in another new direction. My landlord informed me that he had sold the trailer. I needed to move out. Now it was looking like we *should* go to Homer. Where were we going to live if I did manage to keep my coveted job? As far as I knew, the only place possible was the filthy cat/fox trailer across the highway. The owners had taken advantage of me when they kept my security deposit. I had done no damage to the place, but they claimed I did. Absolutely no way I would ever rent from them again. On top of this problem, my contract arrived from Kenai Schools. I still didn't want to move. I waited as long as possible and then I went to pick it up right before the post office would have returned it to Kenai Schools. I signed that I had received it and put it in my backpack. The countdown had begun. Only thirty days left before I had to make that pivotal career and life decision.

More
of
Erik's
Art.

Chapter Fourteen
Homer or What?

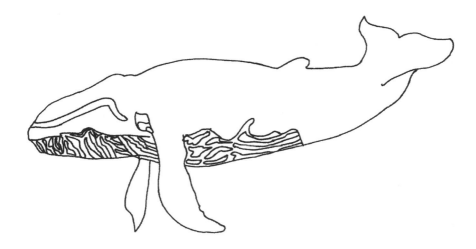

At the end of the month, things really started to happen fast. Diane, and I were arranging work for Erik's first big show. It was scheduled for the first Friday in July, the traditional day that galleries opened up all their new shows each month. In Glennallen, Jeanie, owner of Old Post Office Art Gallery, booked a show for three weeks later. The cards were proofed and sent back several times because of typing errors. Finally Spectrographics started printing them.

The cards finally arrived right after school was over and they still had flaws. They had spelled Erik's name incorrectly. Over and over I had proofed the writing on each card; yet they still misspelled his name. How was I supposed to help him develop his reputation if the printing shop couldn't spell anything, even when given corrections?

Rumors were becoming more and more common that the lady who had been offered a contract for my job was seriously looking for another with Anchorage School District. The best news for me came the day Reed called me to his office and offered me my contract back. Now I had two contract offers. Which one should I sign?

Now that the choice was mine to make, there were so many things to consider before deciding whether to stay or go. I knew that moving to Homer would be perfect for Chris. I didn't think it would be the same for Erik. I would lose control of his art in progress. I knew that Homer was a very desirable location. I had known a lot of Alaskans who wanted to live there because its climate was warmer, it was beautiful, and the seafood was as fresh as could be. There were grocery stores, and good housing, and life would once again be easier instead of the struggle it was in Kenny Lake. No more hauling water at thirty below zero. No more splitting wood after school each night and snuggling up to the wood stove to stay warm in the evening and on weekends.

On the other hand, I felt committed to little Kenny Lake. They had rescued me from unhappy years of substituting in Palmer. Kenny Lake had allowed me to run the fantastic experiment with Erik's program and the district had completely supported us. The staff was so committed and loving. How could I leave any of them? Another important reason for staying in Kenny Lake was the nine-year-old student that I had worked to get enrolled in school part-time. If I walked out on them, they might pull him out again.

When I weighed all the factors, I still couldn't decide. I called Kenai Schools and talked to the high school teacher who would work with Erik at Homer High if we moved there in three weeks.

"Hello, my name is Linda Thompson. I have been offered a job teaching at West Homer Intermediate. I have two sons who would be attending Homer High next year. Chris, my fifteen-year-old is on a 504 plan. He's hearing-impaired and would need extra assistance encouragement to wear his Comtex unit daily."

"Oh, yes. We could help with his accommodations. It would be no problem."

"He also plays Highland bagpipes. Do you know if there are any pipe bands in Homer?" I asked.

"I don't know of any," the teacher answered.

"Okay. My other son, Erik, is severely retarded and is an up-and-coming artist. He has professional shows scheduled this summer in Anchorage and Glennallen. I would like his last year in school to focus entirely on continued development of his art career. What do you have to offer us?"

The teacher replied, "We have two art teachers here. He could take their art classes."

"I am interested in him doing his own art, not doing what an art teacher wants him to do. He doesn't listen to teachers. He only does art the way he wants to do it." I said.

"These classes would be good for him. Both teachers are excellent."

I immediately realized we weren't communicating. This was only normal and understandable, but it was no longer acceptable for me. This situation wasn't what I wanted for Erik. I wanted his art career to continue at the same pace as Linda and I had it going. I didn't want to waste his last year in assignments unrelated to career development. We already had been told that Erik's style was his own, like none other. Why put him in an art class where the teacher would want something else? We were into career development at this point. He could take classes, but he needed to focus on developing and extending his portfolio. Teachers have a curriculum to follow. Since I was a special education teacher, I was free of those limitations. Taking art classes from other professionals might be great at some point, but not that year.

I wondered if the other special education teacher and I had different philosophies. She didn't understand what I wanted and I didn't want to have to train her so she would understand me. I wanted to be in charge of Erik's program and had no desire to hand it over to someone that wouldn't be dedicated to my goals. Of course, if I did want to move to beautiful, warm Homer, I had to be flexible enough to let go and hand some of the control over to a stranger. I needed to keep a somewhat open mind.

"Tell me more about your program," I said.

"We have a wonderful vocational program that your son would fit right into. I could get him a job at Burger King," she said.

That was not what this parent wanted to hear and I honestly don't know what she said after that. I knew Erik. It wasn't even a consideration in my mind.

"But I want Erik to work on his art. I am not interested in him working at a restaurant. He is an artist, and that is where he needs to focus his attention," I said.

She once again continued to tout her wonderful program with fast food restaurants and stores. For some students, it was fine, but not for my son. I immediately knew I would not sign the Kenai contract. The phone conversation had tilted my mental scale toward the Copper River, Kenny Lake side. I knew Kenny Lake would be best for Erik, but I also knew that Homer was what Chris needed. He had not been very happy in Kenny Lake in recent months. Nonetheless, I made up my mind that I had to stay put until Erik graduated in 1999 or even for the rest of my career as a teacher. Erik's needs seemed more critical at the time, and I chose to shape our lives to meet his needs rather than Chris's. At the time I didn't realize a lot of what was happening with Chris. He was continuing to build walls separating him more and more from me. I was a mothering sort of mother, and my fifteen- going on sixteen-year-old wanted more and more freedom. I did not recognize how serious a problem it really was becoming.

I drove to Copper Center Post Office and picked up the certified letter with my contract from Copper River. I stood in the tiny post office at the table and looked at the two contracts, wondering if I was making a big mistake. I couldn't trust anyone else to help me with my dream for Erik except the teachers, aides, and community in Kenny Lake so I signed the Copper River contract and had it notarized by the postmaster. I returned the other unsigned. The next challenge was to solve the housing problem. At least the camper was warm for the summer.

My next stop was to Copper River Realty to see what was for sale around Kenny Lake. There was almost nothing. I needed housing that was available during the summer so I could move right away, since I was ousted from our present rental trailer. The only place I could buy quickly was the cat/fox trailer that we had rented. Its asking price was a small fortune. Another option was to purchase abandoned homesteads but I would have to build a house in two months. That was tempting.

The next week, I drove to all the land parcels that were for sale along the Edgerton Highway. I found two 180-acre parcels that I loved. One had just sold; the other one was worth investigating. It was about twenty miles down the Edgerton Highway. I drove the camper to the parcel with the Copper River Realty sign, laced up my calf-high L.L.Bean boots, checked where the sun was, and started walking through the dense brush. There were places where the forest was old and the walking was easy. There were little hills here and there but most of it had been farmed at some point in the past, thus full of dense, new growth. It was going to cost a fortune just to get a 'dozer in there to build a road. I would have to have Sapa (a local Christian commune that built homes for people) build me a cabin, and fast. It was already June, and I shivered as I remembered the ice in the camper in August of '97. I stopped for a second to consider my options. The forest was so thick at that point that I couldn't see more than six feet around me. The day was warm and relatively bug free. Linda had warned me about bugs in the summer, and yet they weren't bad on this homestead. I wondered why.

Suddenly a thought roared in my head: *Bears here*!

The voice was loud and very authoritative, one worth listening to. I had heard that same voice once before warning me of danger in Palmer in 1995. *I was told to Lock the camper, get in the house and lock the doors.* I didn't listen the first time, and sure enough my camper was burglarized and trashed. I lost my computer and purse that night.

"I've heard that voice before and this time I'm listening!" I said aloud in response. I looked at the sun, got my bearings, and headed straight back to the camper parked on the highway. In five minutes, I was safely inside. I got a popsicle out of the freezer and sat in the warm camper with all the windows open for the breeze.

I sat, munching away and cooling down. My adrenalin-propelled heart stopped racing. I had learned a lesson about listening to those angel voices. "I think I will go talk to the Sapa builders about this place," I said to myself. I started the engine and drove back down the empty narrow road to the commune.

Bill, the man that I had been talking to about building me a house, said, "Let's go take a look at the place." He jumped into his big truck. I led off in the van. Once back at the old homestead I parked on a little gravel pad beside the road that was just large enough for the two vehicles. He pulled in next to me, turned off his engine and rolled down his window to talk. I rolled mine down.

"I'm not getting out," he said.

"Why?" I asked.

"A huge mother grizzly with two cubs was spotted right here this morning. Too dangerous!"

I sat there with an amazed, but not-so-shocked look on my face. All I could think of was thanking God for giving me a guardian angel.

We talked about him building me a cabin but he didn't think he could possibly get anything livable built by August. I was stuck. I had no time. My choices were narrowing.

That night I called Brad of Copper River Realty. I listed all the properties that I had looked at. "Is there anything else for sale on the Edgerton or the Richardson Highway?"

"Yes in Copper Center, but nothing new close to Kenny Lake at this time. The trailer that you lived in last fall has potential. It is actually a good investment."

"The cat/fox trailer? It's a disaster. Well, I have no other options since I am not willing to drive from Copper Center every day. Too far. Could you come down and show it to me today or tomorrow?"

Brad drove down the next afternoon. With the summer sun, I was able to really inspect the property. The trailer was soundly built; the entry lean-to foundation was rotting but could work. I crawled under the trailer and inspected the footings. I jumped on the floor of the trailer and it didn't even shake. The largest structural problems were broken windows, roof damage and entryways. The interior needed to be gutted but I could do most of the repairs. What I loved most was the prime land had drillable water underneath. Water in the Kenny Lake area was a precious commodity. Many well drillers had dug dry holes. The trailer was in the same area as the well for the high school and the fire hall. The land was cleared, and had good hay on it and about $10,000 invested in the gravel road. It had a propane tank and electricity. It added up to more than I had realized. As a renter, it was a mess. As a buyer, I could see its potential.

"Don't get me wrong, I want to make the sale, but Linda are you sure you want to buy? Kenny Lake always loses its new teachers," he warned me.

"They RIF'ed me this year, it won't happen again," I said with self-confidence.

I immediately made an offer for $30,000 less than the owner's asking price. I figured that was what it would cost in repairs. We filled out the paperwork and I drove to Palmer to spend some time in my beautiful home. All the way home I thought about the property. The lean-to was a lost cause since it was rotting from both bottom and top. The plumbing all had to be replaced, though the water heater worked. The water tank was fine. Shower and tub were in okay condition. The toilet needed replacing. The stove and oven were a filthy mess. I would have to scrape for days to clean it up to something I would want to cook on. All the carpet had to go. The list was long but somehow, I would manage to do it all, and Erik's art shows, too.

Two weeks later, Copper River Realty called me to say I could close on the property in a couple of days. I quickly packed up my things, and drove my truck to a friend, who would drive it to Kenny Lake for me. I packed the camper with tools, gallons of white paint, bleach, Kilz, cans of spray insulation, fiberglass, brushes and lots of miscellaneous cleaning/repair materials. After signing at the title agency and paying cash for the property, I drove to Kenny Lake for a summer of construction.

Chapter Fifteen
Reclamation

Upon my noon arrival at the cat/fox house, I unlocked the door and was blasted with the smell of rotting wood and mold. It was the kind of smell that a person always avoids unless she is desperate. I was that. Ugh, how I disliked this place, and I had just paid a small fortune for it. Had I wasted my money? No matter. The place was about to change. My plan was simple; I was going to strip every bit of carpeting off the floor and every piece of fabric off the windows before bedtime that day.

I lugged my heavy tool boxes into the middle of the kitchen, put on my tool belt, and hung from it various-sized crowbars, pliers, and a flat head screwdriver. Then I went to the northwest corner of the den and started to pry up the carpet. The sooner I got that filthy thing out of the trailer, the better. The carpet was rotten where animals had peed in the corner, and it came up easily. Once I got a glove full of carpet, I started to yank and pull as hard as I could. The work was exhausting, and the day was a hot 75 degrees. I soon opened all the windows to cool down and continued on the path of trailer reclamation.

As I went from room to room yanking, sweating, pulling, rolling, cutting, and resting, I made incredible discoveries. The resurrected dirt filled the room with toxic smells and particles that caused continuous coughing and sneezing. I found a fresh package of white face masks in my tool box, adorned my face quickly, and returned to work. The trailer was indeed sound construction-wise, which was a relief. But it was even filthier than I had imagined in some places. After each chunk of shredded carpet was rolled up, I started tearing up the pink pad, using the claw on the hammer on the easy places. In the really dirty places, the carpet was compressed, glued, and shredded into little pieces of foam. The only way to release it was to pry if off with a screwdriver, sharp putty knife or a razor-sharp tool intended for scraping wood. I rolled up the larger chunks and shoveled all the small ones into black plastic bags to be carried outside.

I had no idea that a carpet could have so much dirt under it. There were approximately five gallons of sand and dirt under the living room and den carpets. Chris's room had only about a gallon of dust, dirt, and rotten carpet pad underneath. Under the carpet in the closet were several porn magazines and photos of nude boys from the 1970s or early 80s. I had never looked at a porn magazine. Fascinated, I immediately pulled up a paint bucket to sit on and to read the articles promoting sex, multiple partners, and the free love ideals of the period before AIDS became a part of our world.

Should I feel embarrassed, I wondered? I would never buy magazines like those, but I did find the philosophy of the articles interesting to ponder. How could people expose themselves in such a fashion? How could the writers promote such warped ideas? Did people really believe in what they wrote? I had lived through the 60s and 70s but couldn't relate. Hadn't I heard that this trailer had been occupied by a religious family that used the entryway as a religious bookstore in the past? The irony of it made me chuckle, but on the other hand, looking even at the covers of the magazines made me feel sick in my stomach. I kept them for a couple of days to laugh at with friends who came to visit me and to check on my progress. Then I burned the dirty, creepy things.

Erik's room, which smelled the strongest of cat, had not only sand, but tons of kitty litter under the carpet. Once the carpet was rolled up and the majority of the pad removed, the stink still remained. The wood was covered with multiple layers of disgusting grey-white circles.

Lastly, I approached the smelly entry. It was about 20 feet X 10 feet and held the stairs to the trailer, a 500-gallon water tank, a pump, a pressure tank, and plumbing. The floor was covered in a pile carpet that once had been pinkish gray. It had to go. It was nailed down securely, but the crowbar worked miracles. Within half an hour, I had all the trim removed and the carpet thrown out the door. It already smelled better—not great, just better.

Within a few hours, I had all 1,200 square feet of carpet rolled and the chunks of foam either rolled or bagged. The rolls were too heavy for me to get them out the door. I called around to my friends in search of some teenage boys interested in earning some quick summer money. There were three boys who had an amazing work ethic. One was junior high, and two were high school age. They entered the house as a team and quickly picked up the large rolls of smelly carpet, somehow managed to get them out the door, and threw them in a large pile for the garbage truck. Then we all sat down in the shade and cooled off. I was grateful that I overpaid them for their labors. They left happy. I certainly was.

I called the garbage company in Glennallen to see if they could pick up the pile and haul it to the dump sixty miles away. The truck just happened to be in Kenny Lake that day, so the owner radioed for them to stop by to check on me. About 5:30, the truck arrived, and the driver and helper tossed the heavy rolls into the front scoop and pressed some buttons. Slowly the carpet was eaten by the truck. Life was better already.

I was exhausted, so I went back into the house, hauling a chair and a heavy five-gallon can of white Kilz paint for a footstool so I could sit down to rest with a little more comfort and enjoy the view out the window, even though I was still surrounded by a ton of work. I had just begun. The most disgusting thing about it was the areas where fox and cat urine had seeped clear through the carpet, and soaked into the wooden floor, leaving white circles of ammonia salts from the evaporated urine. This was the beginning of a summer of cleaning, repairing, resting, and cleaning again more every day, one room at a time. I celebrated with each conquered corner.

The two areas that took weeks were Erik's room and the dining room. In the weeks to come, I bleached and bleached over and over. My eyes and nose burned from the chemical reaction set off by the urine and chlorine. Even though I had a respirator on and the windows open, my eyes still hurt terribly. Eventually, it almost seemed clean.

I also tore up all the baseboards around the edge of the house and replaced them with new, clean wood strips. There was no way to scrub or bleach under the 2X4 studs where I was sure urine had also flowed, so I poured bleach all around each upright and base board, hoping it would seep under. That was the best I could do.

My room was the easiest to clean. The carpet and pad came up in one big chunk. With two or three coats of white paint over the dark wood paneling and the dirty beige ceiling, it might even be nice, especially with the large mirrored doors on the closet and the great view out the windows to the southeast and north. I wondered how cold that room would be if the temperature got down to fifty below. It wouldn't hurt if I put my twenty degree-below-zero sleeping bag on top of my bed.

On day three, I started to really paint. I got out the Kilz. It was noted for killing everything that is bad, including mold and mildew. It could be used as a base coat on wood. I had a respirator mask that I wore for safety while working. I had been told by the paint store to always work with Kilz using protective gear. I could get "drunk" from the fumes and possibly hurt myself. It was noted for being dangerous and toxic. Since I was doing all this work alone, I didn't have the option to be careless.

After patching holes in the walls with wood filler, I painted that first coat, and realized that I had made a good investment. The trailer immediately looked better. I could tell that it would be something the boys and I might even enjoy.

The two major expenses were to get the plumbing and heating working. I hired Bob from BJH Construction to fix the water mess. For days he worked replumbing the entire place. The faucets, pump and pipes all needed replacing and the furnace needed massive repairs, but soon I had a working toilet and a bath. While he fixed the system, I painted the living room. We talked off and on each day.

"You sure work hard on this place," he told me.

"I have to. My younger son, Chris, was always sick while we lived here last fall. I want to make sure that doesn't happen again," I told him.

"You're doing a good job. This place will certainly look different when you're finished," he said.

"Well, I hope so."

"If you really want to clean up the air, you must clean out all the forced air vents that run under the house," he said.

"I hadn't thought of that." I went over, unscrewed the floor vent, and took a look at it. It was lined in fur and thick, black, oily goop. "Ooow, we were breathing that?"

Bob came over and looked. "Looks like it. I would recommend you scrape out what you can and then get a vacuum. Take the neck off it and go to Anchorage to buy a long chunk of flexible hose that will attach very tightly. You could hose a lot of it out."

"What a great idea. I'll do it when I go to town to get Erik for his first art show at Aurora."

I did exactly what Bob recommended. Later, with rubber gloves on, I reached in and pulled a huge bagful of pet hair and garbage out of all the forced air vents in the floor. Then, I reached in as far as I could reach and scraped out the gooey mess that coated the inside. For about three hours, with the fifteen feet of new hose and the vacuum cleaner, I pushed, pulled, and wiggled that hose up and down the vents, clogging up two entire vacuum bags. The day the system was all cleaned and repaired, we turned it on, and I was so excited that I wanted to hug this wonderful man. It was fabulous when the furnace worked smoothly and the warm clean air came flowing up from the vents.

After the floor was all cleaned up, I could really see how all the mice had entered the house. I foamed all possible entries. I left the broken front door as it was. I tied the door open for the entire summer and didn't worry about it.

Bob continued to repair the plumbing. In a week I had my first hot shower. It was such a relief to pump water into the 500 gallon house tank and find that it was still there the next day. Showers were wonderful since I was so dirty from all the work. I painted the bathroom and treasured that room.

The work was exhausting and endless. Often, I would collapse onto one of the paint cans or an old folding metal chair that was left by the former owner, and catch my breath. I took my old lawn chair and put it under a big aspen tree behind the trailer to sip a cool pop and take a nap when I was too tired from one job or another. Ah, this is the life, I would think as I relaxed in the shade.

As the weeks went by, I realized that I was not going to be finished before I got the boys back. Erik wouldn't be able to help me, and Chris was so into his friends that he wouldn't be much help either. All the contractors I called were too busy to bother with my little project.

I hired Newly McCoin, my computer geek instructor and a responsible senior. He was wonderful. He knew how to work and do a good job, too. He needed the job and I certainly enjoyed his company. I put him in the kitchen. He scraped out all the mouse feces, then bleached the rotten wood and scraped it down to good wood. He wore the respirator, and I painted other rooms with the windows opened when he Kilzed all the cupboards inside and out. It was amazing how much better they looked after only the first coat. By the third coat of white enamel, the kitchen looked wonderfully shiny and clean. I still feel grateful for the wonderful company and help that Newly was to me that summer.

After measuring each room and drawing up a floor plan, I drove to Anchorage to buy new carpet and pad. I decided to buy short-looped carpet that would be easy to vacuum. I shopped around at some carpet stores, and I settled for some low pile cheap, blue carpet for the living room, the den and the boys' rooms, and white vinyl for the dining room. As Newly worked hard in the kitchen, I cut, glued, and rolled the carpet and vinyl, as the man at Home Depot had instructed. The rooms immediately looked fabulous to both Newly and me, especially after the trim was installed.

The lighting problem had to be fixed. During one of my trips to Home Depot, I found fluorescent shop lights on sale for about $10 each. I installed them in every room to the switchable receptacles. Since we spent so much time sitting at the dining room table, I decided to buy a nice, glass hanging lamp, and it worked wonderfully.

My last large investment was an oil tank, pipe, and a stove for the entry room. I figured that if I installed something that would blow hot air around the water tank and under the trailer during the cold winter months, we just might be able to take a shower at home instead of at school all year. What a luxury that would be! Little did I know just how cold that winter would be.

Both boys came back from Juneau in August, right before school started. Thanks to Newly and Bob, the trailer was finished. I had hung some garage sale curtains, and it suddenly seemed like home. I made up the boys beds' and drove to town to pick them up.

When Chris walked in, he was surprised.

"Wow, Mom, you have put a lot of work into fixing this place up. It looks and smells so much better." He walked all around the trailer, admiring all my work. Erik went to his room and checked it out. He had no idea how hard I had worked to get rid of the urine smell. All the hours and hours of scraping the wood off the floor, and it still smelled a little on warm days. In general, though, the house was immaculate. We were all grateful we didn't have to live in the former hovel.

Children never understand totally the sacrifices parents make for them. I felt a little disappointed that they didn't make a bigger fuss. Did I really think they would understand? They are in their own worlds. I had to think of all the work as something I had done for myself as a person and because it was my responsibility to provide for my children. The place was so immaculately clean that Chris never was sick again. I was grateful that my life was in order for the first day of school.

After being away for the summer, Chris liked being in Kenny Lake. The sun was still up many hours, it was warm, and he was free to mess around with his friends, Tyler, Travis, Newly, and Robert. As soon as he had unloaded his gear in his new bedroom, he was down the road on his bicycle to see them. Life was great at fifteen years of age. No responsibilities.

Erik took his gear out of the camper and unpacked it all in his room. All his boxes of books and toys were already there, so he arranged them in the precise order that he desired. Everything had its place in Erik's room. He never liked to be unorganized.

Chris, never had any sense of organization. His room always looked like a tornado had struck. I would go in once a week and straighten up the piles of schoolwork and books, hanging up clothes in his closet, putting dirty ones in the laundry. Odds and ends were dropped helter-skelter. I was always amazed that he could live in such a mess surrounded by people who were organized like Erik and me. Didn't it rub off on him at all?

We went back to the usual Alaska system of taking off our shoes before entering the house so the place stayed clean all year. Now we enjoyed the roomy trailer each day. It was bright, comfortable, and nice once our belongings were all inside with us.

Hopefully, a nice home near his good friends would help Chris want to stay in Kenny Lake and graduate from high school. He was starting to talk about going to live with his father in Juneau. I was worried. On the other hand, I was very grateful for the "bears here" message. It had inspired me to make the right decision that day. I was sure we were going to be okay.

Chapter Sixteen
First Shows

The summer of 1998, I was rather amazed with all I did. My sister, Cheryl, calls it the year I was driven. I had things to do, people to see, and careers to get rolling besides just cleaning up a 1,500-square-foot trailer. I rarely had time to stop. Some days I would force myself to go outside, sit in the shade of the trees on hot days or in the sun on cool days, and just listen to the birds sing, the wind blow, or the hay rustle in the wind. I needed to get life in perspective. God put us on this planet to enjoy life, not just to work ourselves to death.

In May, the Alaska Chapter of National Downs Syndrome Congress in Anchorage helped support Erik's career. We were invited to give a presentation to the board members and they gave him money, more than $300, for a new scanner for work at home. This has been an invaluable tool in his art career and has been used weekly ever since. We were grateful to the parents who voted this wonderful gift to Erik.

Erik was a Special Olympics athlete, but he didn't train for summer games that year. He did take part in opening ceremonies. Sam Adams of the Seattle Super Sonics outfitted all 300+ Alaska Special Olympics athletes with new uniforms at opening ceremonies. Erik was asked to donate a print that was framed and matted as a gift to him. Diane Louise and Aurora Fine Art donated the matting and framing. That cold, damp, windy June day, Erik snuggled up to me, not just because of the temperature. Here was the frightening situation of being in front of his first large crowd. Nonetheless, when it was time, he stood up and gave the art piece to the big, tall athlete. Erik looked like a little boy standing next to a giant, but the Sam Adams size didn't intimidate him. Erik presented his art in front of TV cameras, newspaper photographers, and about 700 people, many of whom were his friends.

What was most interesting to me at the time was not the reaction of all the non- athletes, but that of the athletes.

One young lady athlete said, "I wish I had people to help me with my dreams. May I shake your hand?"

A young male athlete said, "I am happy to meet you, Erik. I loved your Big Eagle that you gave to Sam Adams. You are a great artist."

Another lady athlete said, "Erik, we are proud of you. You are one of us and you are famous."

The wonderful things these athletes said made a big impression on Erik. He was used to the people close to him praising him, but this was different. All the years of being an active Special Olympics athlete, he had been just one in the crowd. Suddenly, he stood out as a role model for others. He didn't brag or act any differently. He'd glance into their eyes, then look down, and nod very shyly. He didn't have the social skills or language to tell anyone how he felt. He did know he felt proud of his accomplishments as an artist, but to respond with a "thank you," had to be coached by me. When he did say it, it was in a whisper, something able to be read by lip, without a decibel of sound.

The end of June, the Division of Vocational Rehabilitation decided to change their norms and support this developing young artist with equipment that he needed to do his work. They had never done something like this. He had been granted money for supplies and equipment and we had only 24 hours before it had to be spent. We knew exactly what he needed. The grant paid for framing the first ten pieces for art shows, new colored pens and ink, art paper, a wonderful art desk, a professional printer for the IBM computer we owned, and a business plan.

The plan was great that spring, but by fall we had accomplished every goal on the plan. No one expected things to happen so quickly for him. It was amazing, even to me, how quickly his life had turned around. He had a successful art career in only ten months with two professional art shows, prints, cards and brochures of information traveling all around the world.

Only ten months after we first took Erik's tracing paper away and told him to draw, his first professional art show was scheduled for July 17, 1998 at Aurora Fine Art Gallery in Anchorage.

Erik of course flew back from his dad's house in Juneau for the opening. He was quite excited. He got off the Alaska Airlines jet with a look of relief. He gave me a big hug and sighed with happiness that the one-and-a-half-hour trip was over.

The flight attendant who helped him disembark said, "I had a hard time waking him up after his flight. He slept the entire way."

"Thank you for taking care of him," I said.

"He has been crying ever since I woke him. I hope he's okay."

"I'm sure he will be. He falls asleep in cars and airplanes."

"My head," he told me and kept stopping to rub his ears. Tears were running down his face.

"Is it your ears again?" His ears always hurt when he flew. Landings were especially hard because of the change in pressure from the rapid descent.

"Yeah." He was rubbing them while his face scrunched up in pain.

"Plug your nose and close your mouth. Try to blow out your ears gently."

He looked at me but didn't get it.

"Okay, try to yawn like a big camel." I demonstrated a giant yawn.

Soon his face appeared to be more mouth than anything else. He finally stopped.

"Do you feel better now?" I asked.

"Yeah." The tears were still running down his face, but he had a little smile again as he gave me another big hug. I knew that with a few more yawns, he would be back to his happy self. I took a look in his ears and found them all plugged with wax. It seemed like everytime I sent him to his dad's house, he developed ear problems.

After we left airport parking, we drove to Carrs grocery parking lot, unpacked his bag and stowed his things in the camper closet. Then I showed him some of the new clothes.

"Look at what Grandma bought you. Here, try these on, Erik."

Erik took off his slacks and tried on a new pair of black Dockers.

"Erik, look at the new shirt and tie. Here let's try them on." I pulled off his T-shirt and helped him with the new shirt. He couldn't button it, so I did it for him. As I got closer to his neck, he kept tugging at the collar.

"No, not the neck," he said forcefully. "No button. Too tight!" He kept trying to get the collar off his neck. He didn't like fabric touching any part of his neck.

"But Erik, you will look nice with a fancy shirt on."

"No."

"Come on, Erik. Let's just try it."

"No," and again he tried to roll down the collar.

"Erik, come on. It won't be so bad," I said a little more forcefully. He finally gave in and allowed me to button all but the top collar button. He continued to tug at it, but didn't rip the button off the shirt in his enthusiasm to release the pressure on his throat.

"Look in the mirror, Erik. You look nice. Let's try a tie." He didn't know what a tie felt like since he had never worn one. "Look how pretty it is."

As a teenager, I was in the Garden Grove High School Marching Band, the only thing that made high school tolerable. My director, Mr Davis, loved to compete in marches around southern California. We had uniforms with ties, so by the time I graduated I was very proficient in tying them. It had been more than thirty years since graduation, and yet I could still tie a great tie knot on my own neck.

I tried and tried to tie Erik's tie around his neck, but it kept coming out really crooked. I couldn't do it. He was tired of standing and was slowly wilting down to the floor of the camper, making it impossible for me to master the tie. Finally, after Erik was ready to explode with impatience, I took the thing off him, put it around my neck, and tied a beautiful knot.

"I did it, Erik. Okay, let's try that again." I helped him up from the floor and encouraged him to sit on the couch in the camper. Then, I loosened the knot of beauty and slipped it over his head.

I didn't even get it snugged up tightly and he was complaining. One of his hands went to the knot and tried to stretch it out. His eyes squinted and his nose scrunched up. "No!" He tugged and tugged with the other hand trying to roll his collar off the back of his neck at the same time. "No!"

After a winter of splitting my own wood, and teaching physical education, I was no weakling. But even with my superior strength, I couldn't control his incredible desire to have absolutely nothing touch his neck. The battle of the shirt and tie was a match of wills.

Soon his tie was on the floor of the camper.

"No tie!"

"But, Erik, you need to look good. It is your first professional art show," I said.

"No tie!"

I gave up. We finally compromised on a blue and gray polo shirt with its soft, non-binding collar and a beige fishing vest that he loved. He looked casual and clean except for his shoes. "Let's go to Nordstrom to get you some new shoes for your art show. You need to look great for this."

"Okay," he answered as he climbed into his seat in the van, but then started rocking again and was soon not paying attention to me.

After seat belting him, I drove to Seventh and D Street to park the van. "Let's go, Erik." He kept rocking.

"Erik, do you want to shop?" I put my hand on his shoulder and repeated it.

"Sure, I'll go," he finally said.

I hopped out the side door onto the curb, and he carefully climbed out the front seat onto the concrete sidewalk. Hand in hand, we walked over to Sixth Avenue and in the front entrance to the multi-story store with its stylish, skinny manikins and modern art in the windows.

All the shoes in the men's department were too large. Erik's feet were tricky. Like many young adults with Down's, his feet are very short and wide. He measured a size 3½ but men's sizes don't go that small. Women's shoes are the right length, but too narrow. We ended up with a new pair of size five, two-tone green and brown Doc Martens. They were heavy, had great soles, would be good on ice, and would last for the rest of his life. He was ready.

On July 17, 1998, Erik and I arrived a couple of hours early at Aurora Fine Art. Diane had ten different prints framed in various ways and displayed in the back corner of the gallery. The area was small and beautifully arranged on the white walls. Prints were also mounted on white cardboard and shrink-wrapped. Erik's cards were wonderfully displayed in baskets around the gallery.

At 5 p.m. customers were flowing into the gallery to meet Erik. Of course Grandma Behnke and Aunt Melissa Behnke were there too. Grandma was excited and proud. She stayed right at Erik's side while Melissa and I toured the gallery.

"Melissa, look at this," I said. We found a table covered in pizza, punch, fresh fruit, and luscious ice cream bonbons.

Diane walked up. "I thought Erik would love pizza since he talks about it all the time."

"I had no idea you would do something like this, Diane. I'm sure Erik will be thrilled once he discovers he can have some," I said. "Thank you, this is wonderful."

We observed the behavior of the patrons and smiled as people admired Erik's work. Many spent time studying each piece on display.

"Erik, you did all this art?" was the most common question. Many people said, "Your art is wonderful, Erik. It's charming. I love it." Some said, "I love your backgrounds. They look batik. How do you do it?" Erik tried to make conversation, but in general, people didn't understand what he was trying to say to them. Peggy, Melissa, and I helped him communicate.

Erik was most interested in the food table with his favorite, pizza. After a couple of hours, he was exhausted and began teasing all of us. He had eaten enough pizza for three or four grown men. I wisely tried to encourage him to stop eating before he got sick. Once he knew I didn't want him to eat more, he decided it was fun to sneakily tiptoe over to the table and quick grab another piece and start to eat it. It was time to go.

"Diane, how did it go?" I asked, before guiding Erik out the door at about 7:30.

"Pretty good! Erik, your Dalmatian was the first piece to sell tonight. A well-known photographer from New York purchased it. He told his valet to pay for it and take care of the details after he spotted it."

""New York! Wow, Erik, you're going to have art all the way to the East Coast already." I turned to Grandma Behnke and said, "Looks like Diane is definitely going to introduce Erik Behnke to the world." I could hardly believe it.

Erik sneaked off for one last visit to the pizza table before we got him out the door, giggling. He was happy, and Diane and I were very tired. It had been a wonderful and exhausting evening, one I will never forget.

The following Friday, Erik had his second show at Old Post Office Art Gallery in Glennallen. Jeanie had framed the art, and we had paid with the Vocational Rehabilitation start-up money. It was very different from the framing at Aurora Fine Art. We had chosen darker colors for matting, which gave the art a much different look. The black metal frames were all the same size, which gave the matting a different emphasis. I knew things looked different, but I didn't understand why. I had never paid attention to matting and framing before. That day I started really looking at how framers choose their colors, sizes, etc. It can make a big difference in how the art looks. I had much to learn. My education seemed like a never-ending process.

Linda, Syvie, Irene Tansy, and Gay and Dave Wellman all showed up for the opening. Jeanie had ordered a very nice vegetable plate, which the adults thoroughly enjoyed, but Erik had little interest in eating. He did try a few carrots by the end of the show. Someone brought a many layered chocolate cake. Now, that was something Erik really wanted to get his fingers into.

People who really cared about Erik came from all over the valley, but most were from Kenny Lake School. We hadn't felt such love before from a community in Alaska. Like any family, the community was there for us in all ways, including art openings. How could I feel anything but love for this place? I was glad I had decided to stay another year at Kenny Lake School.

Erik was making the news everywhere. Another gallery owner wanted to have a show in September. The owner's response was entirely different from Diane's. Diane had purchased ten of every print he sold. She purchased hundreds of dollars worth of cards too. This owner purchased only three individual prints and a few packs of cards at wholesale rates. I couldn't believe she could even have a show with so little art.

Nonetheless, Linda R., Syvie, Erik, and I traveled together. When we met the owner, I told her I had brought more prints if she still needed to frame or mount them. She proudly took us upstairs to see where Erik's art was hanging. I was shocked. She had framed "Dalmatian" beautifully, but had shrink-wrapped the other two prints and hung them, without mats, on the wall. That was tacky. What actually stunned me was that she had framed $1 cards and had priced them at $59.

Linda and I were amazed, but as usual Linda pointed out something important.

"It doesn't matter. Look, Erik's art is hung near some of the best artists in Alaska. There are $4,000 pieces in here. It's a privilege that Erik's art is even here."

"I'll try to be grateful for that. Now, I really know why people talk about starving artists in Alaska," I said. I managed to sit quietly through the opening. I was very disappointed and tried to think of ways to deal with this owner. I needed to be tactful but that had never been one of my stronger characteristics.

After the show was over, I tried to calmly express my desire for her to sell cards as cards and not as framed prints.

She snapped, "If you don't like the way I run my business, then we won't do business."

She eventually ran out of Erik's cards, and I never sent her any price lists. She did write a year later, but I never responded. If I were going to represent Erik, by golly, I was going to do the best job I could.

I learned a lot that first year as Erik's rep and publisher. I had a lot more to learn, but the one thing I really learned was to hunt for gallery owners who were positive and upright in supporting the artists they wanted to carry in their gallery. Earning money was part of being in business, but being caring and ethical were far more important in the big picture of life.

With the help of the galleries, Erik's art was in Japan, England, Germany, Canada, and across the U.S. by September, 1998. His cards were traveling around the world, and orders were starting to come in across America. We had exceeded our wildest Kenny Lake dreams.

Chapter Seventeen
Survival In Winter

For Chris's entire life, he had been important to me. I loved him more than he could ever imagine. It didn't help that I was a single mom. He became important to both Erik and me all the years of his life. He was Erik's interpreter. He was my best friend and I told him almost everything that was going on in my life. Now when I look back, I realize that I gave him too much responsibility. He needed to be a kid.

The first signs of breaking away had come when Chris turned twelve and didn't want to walk into Palmer Middle School with me any longer. He progressed in his independence, slowly cutting the cord a little more and more each year. As a freshman at Palmer High, he started getting angry with me when I wouldn't allow him to do everything he wanted to do. What did I know? I was just a parent who wanted to control him. He didn't want to be controlled. He wanted to be like Mel Gibson in *Braveheart*. He wanted freedom. He loved the music in *Braveheart* and wanted to learn to play Highland pipes.

We traveled to Europe in 1996, and found a set of ¾ pipes, I bought every beginning bagpipe book the store had and off we went. All over

Europe we traveled. Chris would climb to the hotel rooftops, playing (blasting sound out of) his new pipes. I am sure the other tourists in our group were thrilled by the squawking everywhere we went.

In Germany, I forgot my purse with everything in it (passport, money, ID, credit card) in a restaurant. The driver refused to go back and delay the tour, so on we went. Chris immediately checked his hip bag. He had only $200 US dollars and a credit card that I had put in his bag, just in case. When we arrived in Austria, we tried the card and found that it worked, though I had never used it before. We were going to be okay. The tour company made many calls to recover my purse, but it was difficult to ship from Germany to Italy. The Italians wanted $500 US to ship it to me.

With out cash, or passport, Chris was under a lot of stress. He felt he was in charge. His mother had failed to keep it together, so he had to. When he became frightened, he would start signing to me in American Sign Language and tell me what was bothering him. We became closer than ever.

My purse finally caught up with us in Switzerland, much to my happiness. By the end of the trip in Paris, I was strapping it to my waist daily so I wouldn't lose it. Somehow then, Chris got separated from his hip bag. Someone had stolen it from him. All his money was gone, as was his passport. The tour was over, and we needed to travel to Germany for our flight back to the US. Getting across the German-French border was tricky. The border was closed and guards were checking passports. We decided to cross the border on a train that traveled all night. Somehow we didn't get checked. Next day we made it to the airport in Frankfurt. There was our plane home. We were ready, but airline security found that Chris was pass-portless. I explained that someone had stolen it in Paris. They grilled us extensively. Time was flying by. Every minute the jet was closer to taking off without us. We had only little money by now, certainly not enough to buy new tickets if we missed our free Alaska Airlines mileage ticket flight.

"He is my child. He was born in Anchorage, Alaska, October 11, 1982. I am Scottish and Irish, like my mother. We have to fly home together. We are out of money and must catch this flight. Please let us get on the flight. He is an American and that is an American jet," I begged.

The airline ticket employee yelled, "What kind of mother loses her son's passport? He can't fly without a passport? You will have to go to your embassy and get another if you want to fly on our airline." Security was called.

The security man was softer-spoken but still reiterated the same story. They continued to grill us. I was accused of stealing Chris

Behnke, a German child, from his country. Chris was crying and worried, just as I was.

Chris spoke no German. He bore the German surname Behnke, which he acquired by way of his father and grandfather. That was the extent of his German background. Why were they doing this to us? We were both in tears as the time grew closer and closer to departure.

"No, we believe he is a German child, and you are trying to steal him out of our country," the airline woman yelled at me.

"I am not. I'm an American," Chris said.

They took him away from me, and I became a total wreck. I just sat on a chair and cried. Finally they brought him back to me.

They walked away and left us waiting for twenty more minutes. I was panicking inside and trying very hard to hold myself together for Chris. He was scratching his legs and arms as they broke out in bad hives from the stress and fear.

Finally, just fifteen minutes before loading time for our flight, the man returned. "We are going to let you board your plane. You can declare that you have lost his passport when you get back to the States. It will cost you, but you can go."

Chris and I hugged tightly and nearly ran down the corridors for the departure gate. We didn't dare get more than a couple of feet away from each other for fear of losing each other again.

Once we were happily on the jet, and the door was locked, we sighed with relief. But truly, we never totally relaxed until we landed in St. Paul, Minnesota. Once we were on U.S. soil, we kissed the ground and filled out the forms to pay penalties for losing a passport.

This trip reunited Chris and me as friends. I had never felt closer to him. He grew an inch taller in Europe. We were exactly the same height when we got home. My boy was really growing up. He had saved me and I had saved him. Our trip had been scary, but fun.

In Kenny Lake, he started to grow away from me again. At the start of his junior year, after getting back from his father's, he started talking about dropping out of school. This wasn't an option. He needed to graduate from high school and at least get his bachelor's degree. He was smart. What was this all about?

"But Mom, this school is too religious for me," he said.

"Chris, we have church at home on Sunday mornings. You read the Bible and Science and Health. You're religious."

"Yeah, but they push their religion on the students here."

"Yes, people are religious. Yes, they talk about it. But if you don't agree with them, you just walk away and think the way you want to."

In 1998 many people in Kenny Lake were radical, no question about that. I didn't let it bother me. There were fundamentalist Christians with the billboard accusing any woman who chose an abortion when pregnant of murder. There were anti-NATO signs on the road; there were religious communes; there were people very much against the federal government, or the IRS. You name it, and there were people against it. That was Kenny Lake, but people left me alone and I wasn't bothered.

"Get a grip on yourself, Chris."

Chris felt strongly against the place. One day when we were chopping wood, he said, "I want to go live with Dad and do home school. He said I could."

If someone had photographed me at that moment, nuclear bombs would have been exploding out of my eyes, aimed directly at our state capitol. I was livid with Steve. He shouldn't be tempting this child with an easy way out of high school. Attending Juneau Douglas High School was one thing, but home school, under the tutelage of a father who had never been there for him more that a few short visits a year, was totally out of the question.

"Home school, no way! Home school is never going to work. Your father wouldn't help you enough. You'll end up dropping out. You can't do it alone. No home school!" I declared.

He looked at me with a smirk on his face, like he knew better. More and more, Chris expressed exactly how he felt about everything. He was declaring independence from childhood with his mother.

"I heard some of the boys on the hockey team have been pretty ugly to you," I said. "Lukin has been nice. Hang with him. He is a wonderful boy. Stick with the good guys, and don't let the petty, self-centered ones who like to put others down get to you. That is part of high school. Some people seem to just need to hurt others. I think that is what you are feeling. Am I right on this?"

"Yes and no. I really don't like it when people push their religious ideas."

"Better religion than drugs. It's okay. Is this just an excuse for dropping out?"

"Never mind, Mom, you don't understand," he said.

"The bottom line is no home school. You got it. I have seen all the children doing home school around here. I don't see much quality education happening if the parents aren't totally involved. Your dad is not a dedicated schoolteacher. I will not have this for you, you understand?" I said.

"Yes, but I still want it," he said and walked into the house with a load of firewood in his arms, frowning.

I stood there, shaking. I had won the first battle, but there would be many more on this topic. This child was very headstrong, just like me. Why had his father put this idea in his head? How could a well-educated man even discuss the notion? Didn't he realize the amount of work it would take to stay on top of Chris? I was going to have to apply my old teacher trick of being a broken record, never giving in to the concept. I was going to have to fight my dear son, in a way that I had never fought before. This was going to be tough, and I knew it. I finished splitting the kindling for the next day's fire. Chris and I avoided each other for the next few hours.

School settled into a routine. Five days a week, we all spent long hours at school. Erik's success story was out. Parents started moving to Kenny Lake in search of the teacher who had helped her son become a professional artist. My class load started going up. Each month, more and more students enrolled in Kenny Lake School. By December I had more than thirty students with IEPs enrolled in my class. Would this job ever end? Even if Erik and I stayed until 7 p.m. at night, the work was never caught up. Maybe I had made a mistake in staying an extra year. I certainly would have no more than ten IEPs to service if I had gone to Homer. I was struggling to do everything that had to be done.

Erik's art was flourishing. Chris was floundering. At least I could count on him to keep the fire burning in the heat stove. I was grateful for that. When Erik and I arrived home after school, we would look for Chris. If he wasn't there, we would call Tyler's and he would come home right away on his bike or his skis. Then out we would go to split wood for the night and the next day.

We were a team, and each one of us had a job. I brought in the money, cooked, split wood, and hauled water in the truck. Chris studied and helped with splitting wood or, once in a while, hauled water. Erik hauled the split wood into the house, did his art, and loved us all. We needed each other, and as Chris talked more and more about leaving us at Christmas, I became panicky. I could manage, but the thought of Chris leaving Erik and me in the middle those dark, cold months was frightening. I had become dependent on Chris to help me split the wood. That strong teenage body could easily slice right through all the logs with the maul. I could hit them ten or even twenty times before they split unless I used the cheater (a wedge). Still, it could take me at least six blows to split anything that had a branch in it. The trailer was big and we needed an endless supply of split wood each day to keep the plumbing from freezing and bursting. Would Erik and I be able to manage if Chris left us?

I was loving school, Erik was happy, but Chris kept complaining about having to listen to religious talk in school. It didn't make sense since we had church services every Sunday at home. Erik requested it, and didn't stop until we read Sunday service together.

Eventually, Christmas vacation came. We had a break from school, but the chores continued. Our best discussions came when splitting wood. Doing chores, we had great discussions about politics, the radical side of Kenny Lake people, local gossip, little successes in school like L____, who was finally able to attend school for three hours a day. We were making great progress. Then one vacation day, I lost my battle with Chris.

"Mom, I am not coming home after New Year's. I am going to stay with Dad. We have discussed it, and I am leaving after Christmas."

"Oh, you are?"

"I have done my stint here and I am moving on. I am going to home school and finish my junior year in Juneau with my dad," he said. "I'm sick of this school, I'm sick of the dark, and I've had enough thirty below zero for a lifetime. I want the warm rain of Juneau. It rains there in the winter, Mom. It's great."

"I know you like it. I have terrible memories of that place. Why does it have to be Juneau? I have said it and I will say it again. No home school."

"I'm going and you can't stop me. Dad has a right to see me too. I want to live with him. You've never let me live with him."

Oh, he was starting the guilt trip on me. I didn't leave Steve. I didn't leave him until I was forced into a corner with no future. I wasn't taking the rap for Chris growing up without a father. His father had broken up the family, not me.

"I never wanted to be a single parent, Chris. It was your father's choice. I can see you wanting to live with him. You are a teenage boy, raised by a mom who's done the best job she could. I have taught you how to run a chainsaw, split wood, to build sheds, run power equipment safely, and even to cook a little." I smiled. "Mostly, you didn't want to learn the last thing."

"I'm going, Mom."

"Yes, I suppose I must let you. But, beware. The bottom line is, if I hear that you are attempting home school, I will drive to Anchorage airport, catch the first jet to the capitol, and drag you right back here. Is that clear?"

"Yes, Mom. I still want to do home school though," he said forcefully back at me.

Boy, were we a match. It was time to really start praying about this kid. I was going to have to let go of him, and send him off to be raised by a man who left us in the past. I didn't know what to think. Could I trust Steve with my wonderful son?

Soon, it was time to get the boys to Anchorage, and on the plane to see their dad. All the way there I prayed for God to be with Chris, guiding, guarding, and governing him. Maybe he'd decide just to come home to Kenny Lake in a week or so, but maybe he wouldn't. *Please, God, take care of him*, I prayed as the jet disappeared into the dark. I put my head on the steering wheel, and cried in the parking lot. When I calmed down, I left the airport and drove to a hotel. It would be a six-to-eight-hour drive, and it was snowing. No, I would wait until daylight before I started the drive. I was very depressed, but I didn't want to kill myself by falling asleep at the wheel.

Two days later Chris called. "Hello Mom. I got the part!" he said.

"What part? What are you talking about?" I was sadly already out of the loop on what Chris was up to.

"Soon as I got here, I heard they were having tryouts for *My Fair Lady* at Juneau Douglas High School. I went to the library and checked out the script and music for the play. I studied lines and memorized a couple of songs to sing for tryouts. I'm going to be Eliza Doolittle's dad, Alfred P. Doolittle. He's a drunk. It'll be perfect. I've seen lots of them in the Bush."

"You'll be singing a solo, won't you?"

"Yes. I didn't think I would get such a big part. I actually tried out to be Freddy. I'm really surprised they picked me. I'll sing, 'I'm Getting Married in the Morning.' He sang several lines to me on the phone.

This kid can't hear very well, but he sure has a beautiful voice. I said, "So this means you are going to go Juneau Douglas after all. You couldn't be in their school musical unless you were a student. Right?"

"Mom, as soon as I sang my solo the music director, stood up and said, 'Are you a student here?' I told him I went to Kenny Lake and he said, 'If you want this part, you have to enroll immediately at our high school. I would like you to be Alfred P. Doolittle.' So, Mom, you'll get your way, no home school. I think I will be able to tolerate high school if I can get back on stage and back in music with professionals. I have missed it so much."

I had to admit, Kenny Lake had nothing to offer him in the performing arts. "This is wonderful for you. Maybe it's for the best," I said. "Looks like you were supposed to move to Juneau." Inside I was aching to have him come home.

"Chris, may I come see your performance? I wouldn't miss it for the world. I'd love to hear you sing, dance, and play your part on stage."

"Sure, Mom. I'd love it."

I felt slightly better when we hung up. My life was a roller coaster ride. *Thanks, God, for taking care of Chris. I guess the lesson here is for me to realize that you are really his father-mother God.* You're indeed taking care of your child, aren't you? I was proud of my son.

A week later, Erik flew alone to Anchorage, crying as usual. We sat down and worked on clearing his ears before leaving the airport. Eventually, after the pressure started to release, he stopped crying and started giving me warm hugs.

As we drove home to Kenny Lake, we found that the temperature was dropping. The closer we got, the more the windows of the Subaru iced up. We were down to two little six-inch clear spots in the windshield where air blew up from the engine. We had the heater on full blast, but it couldn't compete with the cold window and the moisture from our breath. The inside of the car was icing up, but the engine kept going, thank goodness. It had to be colder than forty below. It was deadly out there, but we were prepared. I'd learned years before never to travel in Alaska in the winter without twenty-below-zero sleeping bags, heavy winter parkas, mukluks, hats, and very warm gloves. We would be fine.

Eventually, we arrived. We immediately went into the house and started the fire.

"Erik, get your parka back on. I've got to start splitting wood for the night. You need to haul it in," I said.

He went for his parka and other gear and soon followed me out-side. It was so cold that the wood just popped apart, when I hit the logs. My hands froze fast, even though I was wearing warm gloves. They ached from the cold and it was hard holding on to the handle of the maul. Fortunately, within fifteen minutes I had enough split to fill the big woodbox. I stiffly picked up several large chunks and hurried behind Erik to the house. He'd been steadily hauling as I had been working and had left the door wide open. The furnace was roaring, trying to keep the thin-walled trailer above freezing.

"Erik, you left the door open for fifteen minutes. Do you want to break the pipes and freeze the house? It's forty below. Never do that again! Close the door!"

He ran into the house and obediently closed the door in my face. There I stood with my arms loaded with wood, and he had shut the door. It was locked.

"Erik, let me in now. You shut the door!" I called loudly.

He didn't open it. I stood there, looking through the kitchen window, and saw him carrying his wood carefully to the woodbox.

Common sense, oh, how I wish he had common sense. "Erik, let me in!" I yelled. I saw him shuffling quickly back through the kitchen to the entry door.

He slowly unlocked it and opened it for me.

"Oh, Mom, here," he said.

"Thanks, Erik. Just remember to close it again, okay?" I spoke softly this time.

"Yeah, yeah Mom," he said in his normal whisper.

I walked to the woodbox. It wasn't full yet but my hands were frozen, stiff and numb. They were so cold that I really wanted to put my flesh on the metal sides of the stove and warm them up. That wouldn't do. I had to be careful. I no longer had Chris to make sure we were okay. I could not get sick or hurt myself. I was going to have to keep everything together if Erik and I were going to survive the winter.

"Come on Erik, we need to get two more loads to fill the box."

A couple of days later, school closed. The temperature dropped below fifty-below. That was the cut-off for the buses. When it got that cold, the rubber gaskets on motors became so brittle that the oil just leaked out of running vehicles. It was too dangerous for the students to wait in the cold for the often-late buses in the morning. Ice fog wasn't a problem in Kenny Lake, because there wasn't enough vehicular traffic for it to accumulate as it did in Fairbanks, so we still had visibility to drive.

Teachers were still required to go to work even though school was out for students. But neither my truck nor the Subaru would start in the cold. I had put the car in my uninsulated garage and put big thick sleeping bags on the hood to hold in any heat. I had also plugged in the oil pan heater so the oil wouldn't solidify but it was frozen stiff and didn't make a sound when I turned the key in the morning.

While trying to start the truck, I noticed the camper on the back had shifted slightly. I tried to push it back but the heavy plastic cracked and shattered in my hand. "Shoot, I forgot," I said to myself. I should know better than to touch plastic in extreme cold. Now there was a hole in my camper. What an idiot I was. While I was going to college in Fairbanks in 1970, I had seen people break their steering wheels and car door handles when it was below fifty-below.

I missed Chris. Every time I did stupid things, I wished he were there to help me. What if I did something really absent-minded and dangerous? I gave up about thirty minutes later. Nothing was going to start. The Subaru acted dead and the truck sounded like I was tearing the engine apart every time I turned the key. I called Linda R. and asked her to give us a ride. I couldn't leave Erik home alone, so he would have to go to work with me. Her truck stayed in a heated garage and would certainly start.

"I'll be there in about fifteen minutes," she said cheerfully.

I gathered up my schoolwork, put it in my backpack, and called Erik. "Time to get ready for school."

"Okay," he whispered as he walked into the kitchen.

"You can pack your backpack with your favorite books and things. Won't be any other students at school today. Should be fun."

He quickly returned to his room, picked up his backpack, and filled it carefully with his favorite Disney books, binoculars, magnifying glasses, and some Star Wars toy figures.

"Erik, Linda's going to be here any second now. Come quickly and get your gear on," I called.

As I pulled on my heavy bib overalls, two pair of heavy wool socks, heavy men's Sorels (size 10, even though I only need size 7), otter parka, gauntlet mitts, and wool hat to go under my parka hood, Erik got dressed.

Erik wore snow pants, huge Eddie Bauer winter arctic parka, heavy beaver-lined mitts, Sorels, with two pairs of wool socks. I pulled a wool cap over his head as we hurriedly walked out the door.

"Just a second, Linda, I want to check the oil stove and make sure it is running before I leave."

"Sure. Erik, you can sit back here." Linda pulled the seat forward and gave him a helping hand to get my son's very cumbersome body squished into the jump seat of the super cab. By the time he was settled, I was done checking the stoves.

"Thanks for the ride. We could have skied, but by the time I realized the vehicles were frozen solid, it was too late. In this weather, traveling by truck is such a luxury."

"How is the woodpile holding up?"

"Fine. I begged Chris to split a bunch before he left, so I just try to maintain it at about the same level. I don't want to get caught without split wood if I get sick or something. Golly, I miss him."

"I felt the same way when my daughter went off to college."

"I expected him to leave home in a year and a half. I wasn't ready for him to leave when he was only sixteen." Tears still came to my eyes when I thought of him. It'd been over a week since his last call. "I hope he is getting along with his stepmother," I said.

We drove up to the school, plugged in the head bolt heater, and rushed into the high school to visit with the other teachers for a few minutes. Irene Tansy and Syvie were thumping the thermometer with their fingers.

"It's stuck," said Syvie. "I know it's colder than 52 below."

"Mine said 55 below," I said. "It is a higher elevation at my place and should be warmer."

"Mine said 58 below," said Linda.

"Whatever it is, it's cold," said Irene.

"Have you noticed the oil on the ice in the parking lot? The stuff is dripping out of all the vehicles like crazy. If my truck would start, I'd check the oil every time I drove," I said.

It was great having a day to catch up on all the paperwork. Linda focused on her speech lessons. I worked on IEPs. The toilets were frozen again. The maintenance man eventually arrived at lunchtime to try to thaw out the system. Our classroom was pretty chilly, about forty degrees. I left my snow pants and boots on all day. A heavy wool sweater, part of my regular school attire, kept me cozy except for my fingers. They were always stiff from the dry cold.

Linda and I took turns with Erik. He drew black lines and added color to one of his wild bird pictures. Beautiful.

The day flew by.

"I'll drive you two home. I'm leaving soon," Linda announced.

"Pack up, Erik, unless you want to walk," I said.

Linda left to see if her truck would start. A few minutes later, I looked out the door at the truck. It had started and was surrounded by a huge, gray cloud of ice fog.

I checked his coat to make sure he was all bundled up tightly. "Skin freezes in just a few seconds when it's this cold," I reminded him. I put on my cap and pulled up both our parka hoods and fluffed out our ruffs.

"What a luxury to go home so early," I said as we climbed into the truck. There's still a little light out, and we'll be able to see the wood pile when we do our chores tonight, Erik."

Erik and I were getting into a rhythm. I would quickly throw kindling into the wood stove to get the fire going again. Then we'd go around back to the woodpile. I split the logs while Erik hauled the firewood into the house. As I split it, I made little piles, just large enough for him to carry in one trip. I learned right off the bat that Erik couldn't judge what an armload of wood was. One piece or ten pieces of wood, there was no difference. He didn't understand that he had to make many more trips at one stick a trip. Once I figured the proper size pile for him, and gave him directions, he was somewhat independent. I never have understood if he is lazy, or just unable to understand. To this day, he will take one load in and then take off his parka and boots like he is done with chores. I have to keep an eye on him to keep him working. Some days he understood and carried in three or four loads before disappearing. Other days, one was it. That day, he managed to get two armloads into the house before he stopped coming out. I had to keep going until we had enough firewood for the night. Then, I hauled three huge loads in, my back complaining all the way.

I loaded the cold wood into the firebox and then into the giant wood stove and listened to the popping and hissing of the spruce as it caught on fire. I took off my gloves, but felt very little heat coming off the sides or top of the stove. The furnace was roaring.

The Toyo stove was also working hard, blowing cool air under the house. I checked the thermometers around the house; 52 degrees right next to the wood stove in the living room, 41 degrees in Erik's bedroom. The kitchen was 44 degrees while the entry/water room was warmest, at 63 degrees. If it was this temperature at fifty below, we wouldn't freeze. Then I checked my room, 38 degrees with two-inch thick ice on the windows.

That night, after sitting right next to the wood stove and reading a book, I loaded up the stove with wood, turned the damper down just a bit so it wouldn't cause a chimney fire, and went to bed. I put on two pair of wool socks, long johns, and a long-sleeved turtleneck shirt, all under my heavy, floor length flannel nightgown. I climbed into the bed, which was made with two heavy quilts and my twenty below sleeping bag. It felt like the inside of the freezer, so I kicked my feet furiously to build up a little friction and possibly a little heat. The air was so dry that I could see sparks all over the bed from the static electricity I was generating. After a half hour of kicking, I was finally warm enough and fell asleep.

The next morning, the radio alarm went off announcing, "Go back to bed, kiddies, no school today. It's still below fifty below zero."

I smiled. I had no problem having another day to catch up on my work. A teacher's work is never done until the last day of school each year. The winter weather was blessing me with time. I was sure my oil bill was going to be amazingly high, and my woodpile was rapidly declining, but I still had lots of water in the tank, and from the sound of it, the furnace was still working. I slipped into the living room, which was cooling down. The fire was out of wood. I had stoked it at 3 a.m., but all that wood was long gone. There were enough coals left to start a fresh fire, though, without a match. Life was great. Within five minutes I had the spruce popping and hissing again.

I grabbed my heavy afghan off the couch, threw it over my shoulders, and headed for Erik's room, trying to step high. I was wearing wool on my feet, and the static energy produced was painful. Sparks shot up to my feet every third or fourth step if I let them travel less than a few inches above the short carpet.

Zzzzzit, would go the spark. Zzzzzzzzit

"Ouch," I screamed. I stopped in my tracks. "Erik, get up," I called. "Erik, time to get up!" I turned into the kitchen, and got a drink of water out of the big water filter system that I had purchased. Our local water system in Kenny Lake had been labeled unsafe for some reason. No one knew what was suddenly contaminating the water. It had always been safe in the past. I was glad I had put $300 into the drip filter system. Our family had been healthy ever since school started.

"Erik," I called again. Out of the corner of my eye, I spotted him heading for the bathroom.

"Ouch, Ouch," he said.

"Pick up your feet or wet your socks, Erik. That'll stop the shocks," I called. I knew he wouldn't. He hated wet socks.

It was breakfast as usual, and off to school. Linda picked us up again.

We had three days of temperatures below fifty below that week, and then it was the weekend. The road was empty over the weekend. Then, on Sunday, the cold snap broke. I was tired of splitting wood, rationing water, and being shocked on the feet and fingers everytime I touched a light switch. I was ready to go back to school. School didn't remind me of splitting wood. Even though my classroom was as cold (or colder) than my house, days went by quickly at school. I have always preferred to work in the dark, cold winter months. I don't know what I would do for entertainment if I ever retire from teaching.

It didn't warm up very much. It was still thirty below, but that felt like a heat wave after several days cooler than fifty below. Erik and I still didn't need to haul water. Our supplies were lasting much longer without Chris around. He hadn't helped me much in the water-hauling business, but I'll tell you, I really missed him when it came to splitting and hauling firewood.

Chapter Eighteen
Winter To Spring

Winter flew by happily, except for missing Chris. In April, *My Fair Lady* was on in Juneau. I took a couple of days off, dropped Erik off at Grandma's and flew to Juneau to watch Chris. He was great, as I expected. There was something about him on stage. He was a natural, even with little hearing. He had great pitch, if he could first hear the note. Once he had it, off he would go on his solos. There was nothing timid or restrained about him. He loved being up there, playing Alfred P. Doolittle. The crowded audience roared and clapped each time he sang. There were several girls in the audience who screeched the way girls had for the Beatles when I was in high school. I laughed with joy at how happy he was, doing what he loved.

After the show I was introduced to the director of the play, and met Chris's girlfriend. He was happy and proud with his new life and though I missed him badly, I knew it was best to let him go. The next morning I flew back to Anchorage, picked up Erik, and headed down the road, to work on Monday.

I still loved my job, but that spring I was up to thirty-five students with IEPs. I was overwhelmed with all the paperwork. The District gave me another aide to help with students, but it was the paperwork that was killing me. I really wanted to work with the students. There were enough students to justify hiring another teacher, but whenever I suggested it, the administration didn't agree. I started wondering whether I wanted to have a life or teach at Kenny Lake. I guessed I would just have to have my life during summer months. There was no relief in sight.

At times I regretted my decision to return to Kenny Lake School. I had dedicated so much of my life to the school, and my reward was to lose my younger son because of it. Maybe if I had moved to Homer, I would still have Chris, and my life would be easier.

Other times, I wondered how I could ever have thought about going to Homer. Why, without Kenny Lake, I might never have found Erik's artistic gift. Sure living conditions were tough and working hours were long, but we were fine. We'd made it through the winter with all our fingers and toes attached. I was just as dedicated to the job as all the other teachers there. I would stay there for the rest of my career. Surely they wouldn't lay me off again. That wouldn't happen, I told myself, even though the old-timers continually reminded me that the District could RIF me or give my job away again if they wanted to, since I wasn't tenured.

Students were making great progress. My favorite little ten-year-old boy, L___, had caught up with me in height by spring. His hands and feet were far larger than mine. Now he was mainstreamed into a second/third grade classroom and loved it. I often wondered where life would lead him. He had a long way to go and time was going fast. He was almost eleven by then. I loved all the progress he was making in school.

Another of my newer students, a big, handsome high school boy, was living with a relative, who was mean to him. I worried about his safety all the time. He had lost about 30-40 pounds of weight that winter. I was sure he could hold his own, but it was sad that he had to live in that situation. In May, we got him a ride to the Lower-48 to live again with his mother. I was relieved for his safety, and at the same time, I felt the loss of a wonderful child from my classroom.

By late spring, Erik's business and art were really stepping up. His art was still improving, and growing with each piece. He had orders from nine galleries by April of that year. He had almost completed all the work for the poster proposal for the 2001 Special Olympic World Winter Games. Life looked promising for him.

Children were leaving in April, going other places with their families, getting ready for the work season to begin. Two sisters left one week. My class load was declining. Wouldn't you know it though; I had all the IEP and three-year evaluations completed by the time they needed to move.

Then it happened again. Reed called me into his office.

"Linda, I'm afraid I have to tell you, your job has been given away again to another teacher from Glennallen. She's been on sabbatical leave and since you're not tenured, she will be taking your job."

"What? I don't have a job again?"

"No, you don't. But think about it, Linda. What are you going to do with Erik next year? He'll be graduating in a few weeks and no longer able to go to school with you. You will need services, and they will be pretty hard to find out here."

He had a point. I had thought about it many times, but always tried to put that problem out of my mind. What was I going to do with Erik?

I sat there, ready to cry, trying not to. How could they do this to me again? Hadn't I proven my worth? I worked late every night. I had started the first Special Olympics team for that area. I had athletes from Glennallen driving to Kenny Lake for practices. I was good at my job. This district was making a mistake.

"What do you think I should do? Any chance the replacement teacher will act like the last one, and not return?" I said calmly.

"I think you should go to the Alaska Teacher Job Fair in Anchorage and get a good job that will work for both you and Erik. It will be easy for you, with all your endorsements and experience." He said something about me having been a good employee and that he would miss us.

I stood up, with tears in my eyes, shook his hand professionally, turned, and walked out.

Oh, my gosh, I was once again going to be unemployed. I exited the building in tears. I felt totally humiliated, almost as bad as I had in Palmer.

Linda was in the classroom when I arrived. "What did he want?"

"Told me I didn't have a job next year."

"What? You are the best thing we have had here in years. They can't do this to you!"

"Well, they did. I felt angry, and frustrated, but you know what? By the time I got here, I felt relieved," I said. At the same time, tears flowed freely from my eyes.

Linda came over to give me a hug. "What do you mean, 'relieved'?" She sat down.

"Remember last February when I was in Glennallen on school business and I told you to just take Erik home after school, put him in front of his favorite video, and I'd be home shortly?"

"Yes, and Erik didn't stay home. Mrs. Tansy found him wandering down the road without a hat, no gloves, no snow pants, and his coat wasn't even zipped."

"There's no one here to take care of him. I really need reliable care, like that Division of Mental Health and Developmental Disabilities woman told me about last year. It's time. After he graduates, I need to be somewhere that I can hire people to take care of him while I work a few more years toward retirement."

"But I don't want you to go," Linda said.

"Me either. I am completely dedicated to this school district. If we hadn't come here, Erik would be folding towels in the Pioneer Home next year. Now he has a successful career that he loves. I have so much for which to be grateful. I would like to stay here the rest of my life. The district superintendent obviously does not view me in the same light."

"I don't want to work under anyone else. I have seen the best, and I am totally spoiled. I have never enjoyed two years as much as I have these last two," Linda said.

"I doubt that, Linda, but thanks for the compliment." Tears started flowing again and I grabbed another tissue.

"You have been wondering what you were going to do with Erik. This must be the answer," said Linda.

"Guess I am supposed to move again. Geez, after all the work on the trailer last summer! I don't want to go anywhere. I just got the trailer fixed, and the garage built. I have been working on insulating and wiring the new garage every weekend now that it's warmed up. Life was getting better all the time."

We both sat in student desks, quietly thinking.

"I wonder if it will be like last year and the teacher will move on to another school so that Copper River will offer me a contract in June again?"

"I'll look into it for you," Linda said. She called around to find out who the teacher was. In time, we learned the lady was definitely going to take the job. She didn't want it, but she would sign her contract. I really was out of work. There was no chance to stay. I sadly applied to attend the job fair again.

I had to find the right place for both of us. Chris still wanted to stay with his father, so I didn't have to worry about him. Two weeks later, I packed up my interview dresses and suit, briefcase, updated resume and prescreen, and headed off to Anchorage for a few days in the Captain Cook Hotel and the Alaska Teacher Job Fair.

Chapter Nineteen
Job Fair

All decked out in my suit, high heels, hair fixed, double checked that I'd removed all curlers, makeup on, and briefcase in hand, I entered the large room full of tables with signs for each school district. I had made up my mind on one thing: I was going to try for Kenai Peninsula again. I prayed that they would not be upset with my turning them down the year before.

I found the table for Kenai Peninsula Borough School District and recognized Rick McCrumb from the year before. He was busy working with several people at the table. As I approached him, he spotted me.

"Linda, are you looking for a job?"

"Sure am, Rick. I got RIF'ed again by a sabbatical returnee. Need any special ed. teachers? I really only want to work with intensive needs kids; they're my favorites."

"I read about you and Erik in the *Anchorage Daily News*," he said. "Seems that Erik is becoming quite a well-known artist. Congratulations."

"It's been a blast for both of us. We have been blessed by Copper River School District."

"Linda, you've come to the right place. We have openings at Homer High, Seward High, and Soldotna High in intensive needs. I'll book all three principals to interview you together at 5 p.m. today. I'll call them now and have them fly up here to Anchorage for it. Sound good?"

I smiled and said happily, "Yes, of course."

Rick immediately picked up his cell phone and called the principals in their hometowns. I watched in total amazement: from no one wanting me in Palmer to Kenai School District treating me like royalty. I was grateful. I slowly turned away from him and walked through the crowded room to the school district exhibits. Then, I stopped and looked up without really seeing the ceiling of the large conference room.

"Gee, God, Homer is an artist's community. It would be perfect for Erik and for me. Thanks."

Eight hours later, I met the other principals. They were all wonderful. The interview went fabulously well and at the end, they each offered me positions in their schools. I asked for time to think about it. Each had many advantages, but Homer seemed the best bet for us. I had over thirty special education students in Kenny Lake and I'd only have four in Homer. The next day I went back to see Rick.

"I've done a lot of thinking about which opening I would like to have. It's Homer. The school sounds wonderful and it would be perfect for Erik. Maybe I will be able to get Erik's art in a gallery or two down there. There might even be artists who would like to work with him."

"Okay, Linda. I will record your choice."

We shook hands and I turned for the door. To my amazement, the superintendent of Copper River Schools approached me. "Linda, did you accept a job with Kenai?"

"Yes, I did, sir."

"I had been planning on moving you to Glennallen next year," he said, "but it was too early yet."

"Thank you sir, but I think I will take the offer with Kenai, even though it is a cut in pay. I want the security of a job next year and a good safe place for Erik. Glennallen would be okay for me, but maybe not for him. I would like to thank you for the past two years though. Look what we discovered about my son. I really don't believe he would be where he is if we had been in any other school in the state."

"You sure about Kenai?"

"Yes, sir, I am," I said.

We shook hands and parted ways harmoniously.

Chapter Twenty
Graduation

Graduation at Kenny Lake School is a celebration. Thank goodness Linda cared about Erik. I was busy with my other students; I didn't have time to think or plan for graduation events.

Linda always made sure we were ready. Before things started happening she informed us of coming events. "First you need to order Erik's cap and gown. Go talk to Mrs. Tansy about that."

We decided to go immediately and get the order in. Mrs. Tansy had forms to compare announcements and to order the caps and gowns. Two months later the announcements arrived with Erik's name printed inside of each. I hoped that Erik would help fill them out, but he showed no interest. I ended up filling out the lot of them for him and mailing them off to friends and family.

The first big community event was called Leap Dinner Night. It was more than food. It was student's speeches, music, displays of accomplishments and a huge potluck. "You'll love it," she told us.

"What do we need to do?"

"This will be easy. Since Erik is an artist, I think we should display his art. Don't we still have the original framed prints from the art opening in Glennallen last summer? We could hang them."

"Hang them on what?" I asked.

"I'll call around town and see if anyone has a sturdy display. I think Fish and Wildlife has something that would work."

Linda made some calls around the area and found an eight foot tall folding, heavy wooden display made of two-by-fours and plywood. It was perfect. The day before the event, it was delivered to the school gym.

"I think we need to spruce it up."

"It's okay. Maybe if we cut out black paper for a background, and then hung the art, it would look better," she said.

Soon we had a big roll of black paper which we cut and taped up. What an improvement. The black set off the art. We all went home to cook our dishes and change into our fancy clothes for the event and then returned about a half hour before everyone arrived. Linda and I wore our best dresses and fancy shoes. Erik had on a clean dress shirt and we battled over the tie. By this time, he was starting to get used to the idea of tight ties around his neck. He wore it for at least 30 minutes before it was on the floor. We were making progress.

As community members arrived, first they placed their dishes on the food tables set up along one wall. Then they walked around the room looking at the displays built by each of the eight graduating students. The students talked to the people about their accomplishments. Linda and I stayed by Erik and talked for him. He smiled as people admired his art said very kind things to him. He quietly whispered in everyone's ears.

Erik's favorite time for the evening was eating together with the students, staff and community members. It felt like a loving family get-together. Everyone was wonderful to Erik. I had never been to an event like it. Everyone was hugging everyone.

There were many wonderful choices to eat. Pasta salads, salmon, moose meat, caribou meat, casserole dishes made with wild game, potatoes or rice. And then there were all the deserts. He had several pieces of pumpkin pie, pecan pie, chocolate cream pie, chocolate cake, banana pudding, brownies and many other scrumptious cookies. I tried to limit his intake of sweets, but he kept sneaking back for more as a joke.

When graduation day arrived Grandma Behnke, Steve and Aunt Melissa came for the occasion. Chris also came home to help me. During rehearsal, Erik refused to walk into the gym with the others. I knew we were going to have a battle on our hands with him. I didn't want to have to lead him around in front of the whole community and hoped he would cooperate that evening.

All eight graduates were wearing their rich blue caps and gowns and were waiting in a classroom. Everyone was encouraging and helping each other look their best. Finally, the time was near. The gym was packed. Almost the whole town came. The bleachers were full of folks in their everyday wear, and the seats on the floor, set up for family members, were full of people all dressed up in their best outfits. Women wore dresses from cotton to silk and all different hem lengths and men wore suits and ties. Pretty ritzy for Kenny Lake.

Chris volunteered to help me with Erik and was standing about thirty feet down the route that Erik was to walk. If he wouldn't go, I would signal Chris. He would go escort Erik through the crowd of people and up to the little stage where all the graduates were to be displayed for the crowd.

The first three graduates came out, walking one by one to the beat of the music played by the very small school band of six assorted instruments. But when it was Erik's turn, there was absolutely no way anyone could get him to step forward in front of the community. It was by far the largest crowd Erik had seen all winter. I signaled to Chris, and he calmly walked over to Erik, grasped his hand, and spoke encouragement to him. Soon the two of them were marching through the gym.

Erik was very upset. As he walked around, he had one hand firmly grasping his brother's and in the other was a beautiful yellow rose. His huge bottom lip was sticking out, illustrating his lack of desire to be a participant in the event. Slowly, Chris led him through the crowd and up to his chair on the yellow and blue balloon-trimmed stage. Chris helped him walk across the stage before he left him sitting in his proper seat. I was proud of both my boys: Erik for graduating and Chris for being such a wonderful brother.

Once Chris left his side, Erik sneaked a look at the audience, spotted Linda R. and me and we all smiled at each other. He gave us a thumbs up and we returned it to him with beaming smiles. Linda and I were proud of his accomplishments.

Ben Stevens, our Senator Ted Steven's son, announced that Erik had been chosen to be the official artist for Special Olympics. He unveiled a proposed proof of Erik's art.

"I would like to present an award to Erik David Behnke for his talent, contribution, and dedication to the arts. His work will be used to help promote the largest sporting event in the history of Alaska, the 2001 Special Olympics World Winter Games."

He presented Erik with a two-foot by three-foot draft of the poster of Erik's art. Everyone clapped, and some people even stood up and hooted loudly for Erik as the large placard was handed to him. He smiled contentedly, but didn't completely understand what was happening to him. Elishia Cook, a graduate sitting next to him, tried to explain it. Finally he smiled proudly and nodded at everyone. Erik was the artist for an international event. It was quite an honor.

Scholarships and awards were given out to the students, speeches were made, and soon the ceremony was over.

After that, everyone cheered and a long line of people soon formed for refreshments. The tables were covered in blue and gold paper with balloons and crepe paper streamers. There were many plates full of delicious homemade cookies, cakes, puddings, and wonderful punch to drink. Each graduating student had an individual table where people put presents for them. Linda led Erik and me to his table, and people crowded around and encouraged him to open each of the gifts in his pile. Everyone was excited to give and share what they had with the graduates. The laughter and joy of the evening was heartwarming for all. Erik received a statue of a cartoon character wearing a cap and gown. Mrs. Tansy gave him a wonderful print of sled dog puppies. Some people gave him prayer books, little journals, an address book and other presents. Children were running everywhere; everyone was congratulating the graduates.

When folks started to leave, several of us stayed to clean up the gym. All the chairs and tables were washed and put away, the bleachers were pushed back into the wall, leftover food was shared, and the floor was swept and mopped where needed.

That night, Erik happily said as he went to bed, "No more school, Mom. No more school!"

Chris had to help Erik walk into graduation ceremonies. Everyone from the region was there and it was too overwhelming for him. With his brother at his side, he was able to walk the pathway through the crowds and up to the stage.

There were eight graduates for the class of 1999. This is was the moment where the tassels were turned to the right side. Elishia Cook, the wonderful girl next to Erik, assisted him.

149

During graduation ceremonies, Ben Stevens, director, presented Erik with a draft of the poster using his art that would be used in the 2001 Special Olympic World Winter Games. This was the largest sporting event in the history of Alaska. Erik's art was used in all the advertisements in papers and magazines, on the sides of the buses, on the poster, and on the front cover of the cookbook for the games. His art traveled around the world with the athletes after the games were over.

Reed Carlson handing Erik his graduate packet and shaking his hand. Erik always felt comfortable around Reed and loved to watch the fast dashing principal play basketball during lunch at school. (above right)

Erik with his graduate packet. He did not get a diploma because he was not able to take regular mainstream classes like English, science, history. He has managed to be successful, even without the document. (above left)

Chapter Twenty-one
Homer and Beyond

Once school was over, I drove the camper to Homer to arrange for a place to live. I couldn't decide what to rent, but a friend knew of a duplex going on the market. I was able to walk through one apartment to see what it was like. Young wanna-be hippies were camping out in it, and even though it was very dirty, the building appeared to be in sound condition. It had running water, oil heat, six-inch-thick insulated walls, large windows looking out at world famous Kachemak Bay, and a gravel road to the property. On top of that, it was relatively private, considering it was in a town as large as Homer, population 5,000. I agreed to purchase it and the owners agreed to finance it.

In July, my sister Cheryl flew up from California to help us move everything from Kenny Lake. We packed up a huge U-Haul truck and I drove it across 500 miles of winding roads in two days. Chris drove the van and we camped in it. Once at the apartment, we tore out all the dirty carpeting and one wall, enlarging the living room. We painted everything white, and repaired little things. In three weeks we were content. That little 1,100-square-foot apartment was comfortable for two years, but eventually, because Brown Bear Products, our art business, grew to have thousands of prints, cards, posters, framing materials, glass, packing materials, Erik's *Alaska Animal ABC Coloring Books* and a web site, we needed more room.

After four years, I sold the duplex and my beloved Kenny Lake property piecemeal but kept my Palmer house as a rental. Erik and I bought a wonderful solar home right on beautiful Kachemak Bay. We enthusiastically watch the seals, sea lions, pheasants, eagles, moose, bear, and thousands of other creatures year 'round. The home has a floor for Erik's studio and Brown Bear Products business, and two more for living. The three garages are needed to store the covered trailer, displays, tables and other gear that are used for art shows and fairs year 'round.

I still teach intensive needs special education, coach Team Homer Special Olympics, run the business (Brown Bear Products), maintain www.erikbehnke.com, actively promote Erik's art, do art shows almost every summer weekend, lecture at conferences, work as a parent advocate nationwide, and write. My beloved Chris comes home occasionally, and calls monthly. He is happily off on his own adventures now, like his mother at his age, and learning more and more about Irish music and Uilleann (Irish) bag piping. Though he loved theatre performance, he did not pursue it as a career after he graduated from Juneau Douglas High School in 2000.

Erik's career continues to grow and develop. He is always in eight to ten galleries around Alaska. He has had many shows in Alaska now. Galleries and stores in Homer, Anchorage, Ketchikan, Valdez, Chitina, Fairbanks, and Juneau are pleased to carry his work. He has had shows in Seattle, Boston, Washington D.C., Denver, Phoenix, Spokane, and Kansas City. His art is now in many countries all around the world. His unique style is well-known. His story has become an inspiration to both people with and without disabilities. He gives people hope for a better future.

Epilogue

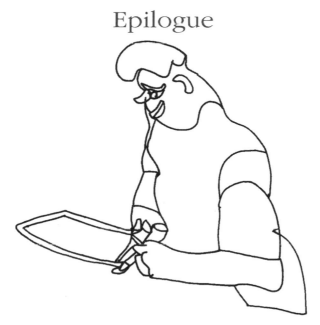

Three log benches surrounded the campfire on the grassy cliff. Burgers, hot dogs, and steaks sizzled and popped in the open flame off the spruce wood fire. Smoke drifted off toward the big beach house to the north.

"I assume your favorite food is still hot dogs, Chris?" I said.

"Mom, I ate hot dogs because I was hungry and didn't want to bother to cook. Besides, I am a vegetarian now."

"You are? Oh!"

"Erik, how about you? Want anything?" I asked.

He picked up a bun off the plate and said, "Oh, yeah, yeah."

"Burger, dog, or steak?"

"Burger," Erik whispered. I placed the meat on his plate. Smiling, he carefully poured ketchup, mustard, and relish from squeeze bottles onto the bun. I rolled the dogs over and flipped the sizzling steaks.

"I heard in Juneau that Erik had art shows in Washington D.C., and Kansas City," said Chris.

"They were all a blast. In D.C. we met artists from around the world. In Kansas City, Erik won 'Best Professional Artist'. He has a show in Seattle, and another in Phoenix in the spring. I love traveling to his openings."

"Chris, are you still upset with me about taking you out to Kenny Lake?"

"Mom, Kenny Lake was wonderful, now when I look back on it. I made good friends and had a great adventure. If we had stayed in Palmer, I probably would have left you there too. I needed to go. If I had stayed in Palmer until graduation, I wouldn't be the person I am now."

"How about your music?"

"I'm working this summer for the U.S. Forest Service and when the job ends in October, I'm still planning on going to Ireland to work with some really good Uilleann pipers. I love playing. It's all I want to do, Mom."

"Don't you practice your Highland pipes anymore?"

"No, the fingering is much different and it gets too confusing. The Uilleann pipe sound is what I love."

"You know, having you and Erik has been my greatest adventure. I'm grateful that you both survived our lifestyle. I love you both so much."

"I wouldn't trade my childhood. I was pretty frustrated at sixteen, but I'm not now. I love you too, Mom."

"Thank God teenagers do grow up!" I said with my hands over my head as if I were praising the Lord in a tent revival.

We stopped talking and watched three eagles sail nearby with their five-foot wings wide, catching the updrafts off the cliff. The swallows dashed all around us with their green wings flashing silver as they turned. Seals could be heard barking off in the distance.

"Mom, I sure would like one of those juicy steaks," Chris said.

"I thought you were a vegetarian."

"I was joking."

"Well, here you go. Got to spoil ya when I can. Tomorrow you'll be off on more adventures, just like I was. Enjoy," I said.

"This place is incredibly beautiful. I love it here."

"Me too. I love our big warm home and the view. It's to live for." We all three stopped eating to look out over Kachemak Bay where the wind gently rippled the water.

"Life is a wonderful adventure," I said.

"Yeah, you're right on that one," said Chris. "It has many possibilities."

Erik looked lovingly at the two of us and smiled. It was good to have the family together, even if it only was for a short visit.

We sat around the campfire, stuffing our faces with all the good food, enjoying the view and each other's company. Life is interesting, and definitely worth living.

Children, they certainly have changed my life.

I never would have dreamed that I would have the wonderful life I have now.

I am grateful to have been blessed with my boys.

Erik standing in front of part of his display at an art opening at Aurora Fine Art in Anchorage, 2001.

Part of the display at Zoez Window Gallery in Anchorage, 2000.

Erik standing during his show at the entrance to Aurora Fine Art, Anchorage, with the Special Olympic World Winter Games poster on the door to the gallery, 2001.

Erik standing with his display of art during the Art Potpourri at the Anchorage Museum of History and Art.

Erik standing with one of the enlargements of The Snow Boarder. All eight images were enlarged to 3 feet by 4 feet in size and hung in various locations during fundraisers around Anchorage before the World Games.

Chris Behnke (top) Erik Behnke (middle) and Linda Thompson (mom) in a family photo taken in 2002. Chris had grown up and was attending college at the time. (right)

Erik on the porch of our home on Kachemak Bay relaxing on a summer day. He was taking a break from working on his art. Homer, 2006. (below)

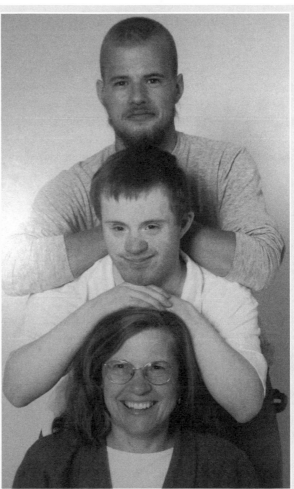

Erik relaxing in our house in Homer, 2005. The downstairs of this house is his studio and framing room for his art.